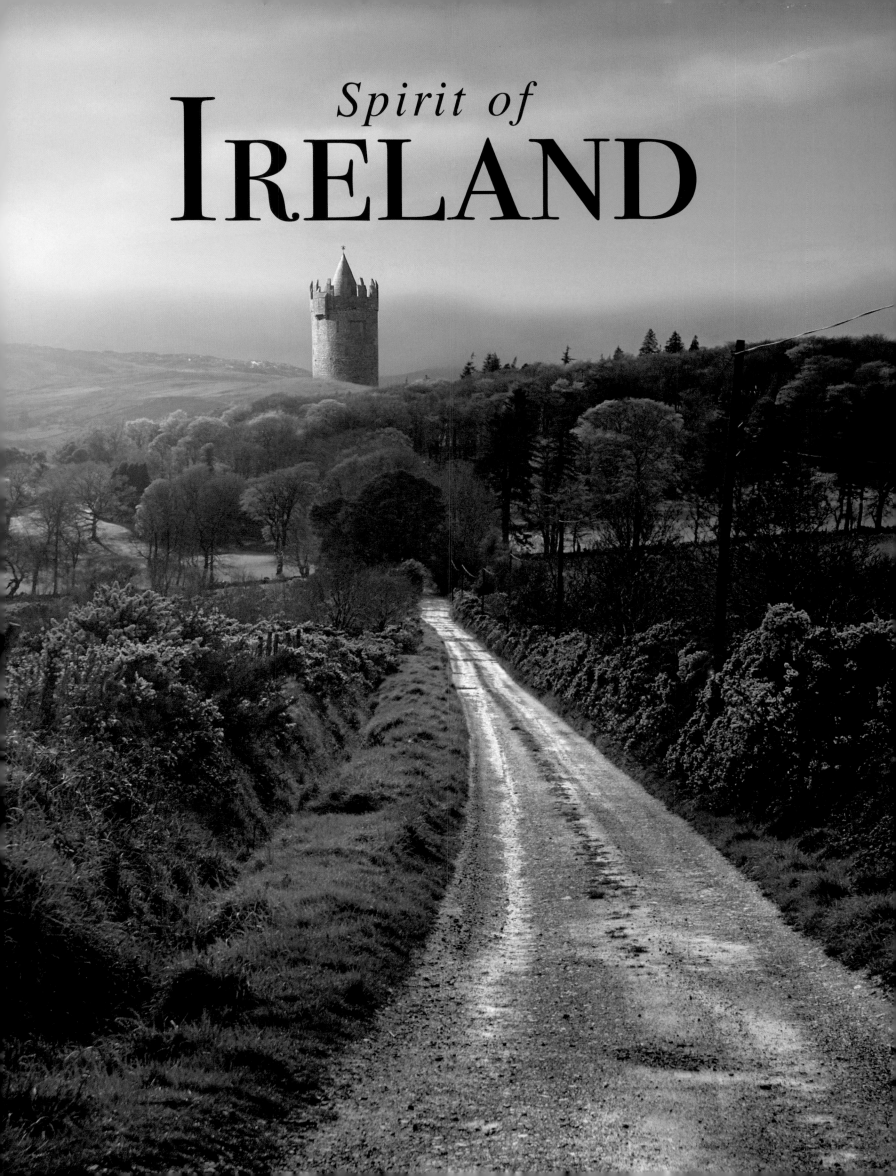

Spirit of
IRELAND

Spirit of
IRELAND

PaRragon
Bath · New York · Singapore · Hong Kong · Cologne · Delhi · Melbourne

First published by Parragon in 2008

Parragon
Queen Street House
4 Queen Street
Bath BA1 1HE, UK

Designed, produced, and packaged by
Stonecastle Graphics Limited

Text by Gill Davies
Designed by Paul Turner and Sue Pressley
Edited by Philip de Ste. Croix
Picture research (Corbis) by James Stringer
Additional picture research by Harry Sharp and Karen James

ISBN 978-1-4075-5570-6

Printed in China

Page 1: There is always something interesting just around the corner in Ireland: a glimpse of sparkling sea or lake, a beguiling inn — or an atmospheric castle turret such as this.

Pages 2-3: Those lost in the Irish Potato Famine in the 1840s are not forgotten. At Doo Lough Valley, County Mayo, a lonely wayside stone monument set beside the azure lake is dwarfed by steep mountainsides but still captures the attention.

Pages 4-5: Alluring islands rise magically through the mists, redolent of past mysteries and magic tales.

Contents

INTRODUCTION

Ireland's national symbols are the shamrock and the harp: the first one represents the luck of the Irish, a touch of magic, and the mystery of the Holy Trinity — Saint Patrick reputedly used the shamrock's trefoil leaf as an illustration to explain this doctrine. Even before the Christian era, the shamrock was a sacred plant to the druids in Ireland because its leaves formed a triad — three has long been a mystical number for the Celts and, moreover, the shamrock's triple leaves, amazingly, stand upright to warn of an approaching storm.

The other emblem, the harp, has represented the music of Ireland and its people since the 13th century and Ireland is the only country in the world with a musical instrument as its national symbol. It has been used on Irish coins ever since those minted during King John's reign (1199–1216) and is still seen on today's Euro … as well as on Ireland's coat of arms and official seals (including the Great Seal of the Irish Free State) — and on passports. It even serves as the Guinness trademark. The oldest surviving example of the real thing is the Brian Ború harp that dates back to the late 14th century — it is now preserved in Trinity College Library, Dublin.

A land of legend and history

Ireland's story dates back way beyond comparatively recent medieval times to an ancient past, the influence of which has percolated through to today in many a legend — some recorded by monks, others told or sung to willing listeners through the ages. Collectively they form part of Ireland's rich storehouse of myths and histories. Built long ago, beyond the shrouding mists of recorded history but still stout and very visible reminders of ancient times, stand the austere stone circles and monuments raised from about 6000 BC. This is an ancient land where druids and mysteries once held sway — an island that would later be invaded by the Viking Norsemen who settled in the country and seized power from the late 8th century until King Brian Ború defeated them at Clontarf in 1014. Ireland had been converted to Christianity by Saint Patrick in the 5th century. Saint Patrick is the patron saint of Ireland, and he embodies Irish traditions that are now celebrated with gusto, both there and abroad, on Saint Patrick's Day on 17 March.

This is an island where the past has left imprints everywhere — in age-old tales, in castles and dolmens, in the

Left: The harp has appeared on Irish coins since the 12th century.

Above: The emerald shamrock, a symbol of the Irish nation, of the Holy Trinity, and Saint Patrick's Day.

Opposite: This 4500-year-old portal tomb is named Legananny, after Liagán Áine, a mythical goddess loved by giant Finn McCool.

sun spirals carved on ancient tombs. These traces have become an intrinsic part of the breathtaking scenery where wild waves churn and spit against rugged sea cliffs that ring the west coast of the island, where purple heather-clad mountains rise majestically above rippling lakes and mysterious marshes to meet a cloud-spun sky that washes them with soft rain, keeping hills and fields as green as the precious gems that lent the Emerald Isle their name.

Coastal fringes

In the east, the Irish coast lies tantalizingly close to Scotland and Wales but in the west it is a remote place, far removed from anywhere else in the world — for here the jutting headlands and promontories face the mighty North Atlantic Ocean with uninterrupted passage to the Americas. In times past many impoverished emigrants left these western shores, seeking a new life elsewhere, far across the wild waves. If these voyagers could have looked into the future, they would perhaps have been surprised to know that in the 21st century, Ireland would become one of the wealthiest nations on the globe! Moreover, many of those who left (or their offspring) did, quite literally, make their fortunes in the New World. As the Northern Irish author, C.S. Lewis (of *The Lion, the Witch and the Wardrobe* fame) once remarked, *Failures are fingerposts on the road to achievement.*

Back on the Irish shoreline, the seabirds soar above, wheeling back and forth, crying plaintively where Ireland's rugged rim vanishes into the ocean. Seals cavort along the rocky coast as turtles, dolphins, and whales cruise by headlands pinpricked with pink thrift and milk-white sea campion, with many ancient castles or forts crowning nearby summits. Beyond the cliffs and windswept beaches, the high sea stacks and caverns, a plethora of inland wildlife waits — glistening salmon leap in the rivers and surge up gushing waterfalls, falcons and owls spy on playful fox cubs as badgers, otters, and squirrels scurry about their business. Rabbits, hares, and deer prick up alert ears and then vanish into the lush trees or tall grasses.

Right: The beautiful Ring of Kerry presents a splendid panorama carved out of rock during the last Ice Age some 10,000 years ago with mountains, cliffs, sweeping beaches, and many inspiring views. This area encompasses much of the typically ancient heritage of Ireland including Iron Age forts, stone circles, and Ogham stones carved with ancient letters. There are castles, holy wells, and monastic dwellings — abbeys, friaries, and beehive cells — set astride fingers of land wrapped by a sparkling blue sea.

Left: Here lie calm stretches of water while purple gray mountains rise all around, with field and hill seamed by huddled stone walls. Sheep graze contentedly beside the lakes and ribbons of road.

Below: Music with pipes and guitar, convivial drinking, fun, and enjoyment — all on offer in many cheery pubs in Dingle, County Kerry, like Murphy's down by the seafront.

Many merry tales

Threading throughout the landscape, twisting roads and lanes lead from the country to numerous vibrant cities, such as historic enchanting Dublin, ancient hilly Cork, medieval Limerick, lovely Galway, and bustling Belfast. In every town, port, village, isolated farm, and homestead live some of the most beguiling people in the world, renowned for their wit, charm, and poetic lilt. They will tell you tales of leprechauns disappearing with their rocks of gold and of the many Irish fairies and ghosts, of the thunderous giants who built the great basalt jumble of the Giant's Causeway (now under threat by rising sea-levels). They will remember the sometimes bloody past, the bravery and the heroes; they will entertain you with their wry jokes and then enchant you with music and melody as harp, pipe, and fiddle soothe or chase away cares in many a cosy pub.

As the Irish poet W.B. Yeats memorably wrote in 'The Fiddler of Dooney':

For the good are always the merry,
Save by an evil chance,
And the merry love the fiddle,
And the merry love to dance.'

… And, for sure, Ireland is the place to do it!

CHAPTER 1

THE COAST OF IRELAND

Purple mountains and emerald hills sweep down to embrace an amazingly varied coastline. There are sandy beaches where placid waves curl white-edged or silver in the moonlight, lapping as softly on the shore as the gentle lilt of Irish poetry or the sweet harmony of harp strings. In sharp contrast, elsewhere jagged cliffs tower above savage rocks where the ocean hurls itself in a frenzy — pummeling the coastal fringe in a wild dance like an angry giant. Everywhere seabirds wheel above sea stacks and caverns and over the populated areas that are alive with picturesque harbors and colorful fishing boats.

Above: *A serene sea ripples gently over Inch Beach, Dingle.*

Left: *Wild waves lash the jagged rocks of a coastal promontory.*

The coastline of Ireland is some 3500 miles (5600km) long. It is deeply indented in the west and with slightly smoother contours along its eastern edge. Waves crash wildly on rugged shores or gently caress soft sands. Behind the shoreline loom purple heather-clad mountains or rippling green hills where soft rains fall. Everywhere the bright shining grass is a reminder of how the Emerald Isle earned its name. Here are windswept headlands, solitary lighthouses, many ancient castles and forts, and cliffs dotted with clumps of thrift and sea campion.

Surrounded by water

Ireland is separated from the British mainland by the Irish Sea, the North Channel, and St George's Channel. The Irish Sea *(Muir Éireann)* is an arm of the North Atlantic Ocean, bounded by Scotland to the north, England to the east, Wales at its southern extreme, and Ireland on its western flank. It occupies some 40,000sq miles (103,600km²), stretching about 130 miles (209km) in length and 140 miles (230km) in width. It is connected with the Atlantic by the North Channel's brisk waters that slice a passage between Northern Ireland and Scotland, narrowing to a mere 13 miles (21km) between Scotland's Mull of Kintyre and Northern Ireland's Torr Head. The Irish Sea runs northwest to southeast, with lighthouses on several Scottish isles warning vessels to keep their distance from the hazardous shoreline. Situated on the east coast of Northern Ireland, Larne offers the shortest, fastest shipping routes across the Irish Sea to and from Scotland.

To the south, St George's Channel meets the Irish Sea between the coasts of Wales and Ireland. Here ferries arrive at

Above: Dún Laoghaire lighthouse, one of a pair that guide ships safely into harbor before they proceed onward to Dublin port.

Right: With sandbanks and sharp rocky outcrops, the treacherous waters of Dublin Bay have been the scene of many shipwrecks.

Dublin and Dún Laoghaire from Holyhead (in Anglesey, north Wales) and Liverpool, where the 'pig's head' shape of Wales butts up against northern England. These are often turbulent waters that have a reputation for reducing landlubbers to a few hours of wretched seasickness, although sometimes the Guinness knocked back at the Irish bar may also have had a part to play!

The southwestern end of St George's Channel merges into the Atlantic Ocean. This strait is some 100 miles (160km) long and 50 to 95 miles (80 to 153km) wide, separating southeast Ireland from Wales. At its narrowest point, a short but gusty 47 miles (76km) of sea tosses its white-peaked waves between Carnsore Point (near the Irish port of Rosslare) and historic St David's Head in Wales. Many vast ferries and smaller hovercraft bustle between the ports of Fishguard or Pembroke (both in south Wales) and the Irish port of Rosslare, taking passengers, trucks, and cars across the sea. This stretch of water was named for the legendary Saint George, of dragon-slaying fame, who was said to have voyaged to Roman Britain across this channel. Today those living on the tip of the Pembrokeshire coast claim that on a really clear still day, perhaps once every five years or so, the coast of Ireland becomes visible as a deep purple ridge where turquoise water meets the sky.

Facing the Atlantic Ocean

Ireland's west coast bears the full brunt of the mighty Atlantic Ocean. From the Dingle peninsula, traveling due west, no other landmass breaks the water until Newfoundland in Canada. For more than 6000 years this mountainous headland jutting into the sea has been a home to people who have either tolerated or relished the isolation of this rugged area. Long ago, tribes raised over 2000 monuments in this remote location overlooking the vast blue ocean.

The Atlantic is named for Atlas, the giant Greek god who bore the weight of the world on his shoulders. It is indeed huge, second only to the mighty Pacific and, with its adjacent seas, measures some 41.1 million sq miles (106.4 million km²) in area, occupying about one-fifth of the globe's surface. It wriggles north to south like a rather plump S-shape between Europe and Africa on its eastern fringe with the Americas far beyond to the west. Of course, in pre-Columbian times, its distant western waters were believed to be lapping at the edge of the world plate, off which foolhardy sailors would surely tumble if they sailed too far.

Gas and oilfields lurk below the ocean's surface while water from the Gulf of Mexico is carried by the swift and powerful Gulf Stream right across the Atlantic to join the North Atlantic Drift and travels on to Ireland, this temperate flow warming its coastal climate and encouraging fish stocks.

Above: In May and June drifts of thrift, sea campion, and birdsfoot trefoil flourish on the Dingle peninsula.

Right: As the tide retreats, a gleaming beach reflects the golden and blue patched sky, drifting clouds, and the silhouette of a solitary rider beside the edge of the Atlantic Ocean.

Coastal wildlife

Many sea creatures live in the cool clear waters between Wales and Ireland, enjoying ample meals of smaller fish fry. Here bottlenose dolphins, porpoises, basking sharks, Atlantic gray seals, lobsters, and leatherback turtles swim.

Leatherback turtles *(Dermochelys coriacea)* are huge: the largest sea turtles in the world, they may weigh a ton and measure nearly 10ft (3m) in length. They have been swimming mighty distances through our oceans for some 100 million years and are the only reptiles that generate their own body heat. Despite their vast dimensions, they survive on what seems like a rather insubstantial diet of watery jellyfish, of which there are plenty in the Irish waters. They gather here every year to feast after covering huge distances from the waters of places like Brazil, Suriname, and French Guiana.

Researchers believe that leatherbacks are likely to become even more common visitors to the seas around Ireland — simply because the water is getting warmer due to climate change.

Marine wildlife

Ireland's varied marine life includes bluefin tuna, conger eels, turbot, and whales. In the early 1990s the Irish government declared the coastal waters of Ireland to be a whale and dolphin sanctuary. This summer feeding area for visitors is home all year round to the harbor porpoise while the south coast is a good place to spot fin, humpback, and minke (or little piked) whales. These latter are small by whale standards at about 30ft (9m) in length — they are just one of 24 species of whales and dolphins recorded in Irish waters seeking the plentiful shoals of fish close to shore. Many cetacean species have been seen recently in the clear unpolluted waters off west Cork, making this one of Ireland's richest sites for whale watching. Minke, fin, and humpback whales arrive here from May onward and right up until the early winter they may sail by close to shore as do long-finned pilot whales, common dolphins, sometimes bottlenose and Risso's dolphins and, occasionally, killer whales (actually a species of dolphin).

Above right: One of the most important concentrations of bottlenose dolphins in Europe is found around Ireland's west coast, with the Shannon estuary home to the only known resident group in Irish waters and one of only six such groups in Europe.

Right: When they breed, leatherback turtles travel to warmer places (like the Caribbean, French Guiana, and Brazil) but in between amorous rendezvous, these vast turtles enjoy feeding in the cooler waters around Ireland, trawling for their favorite jellyfish.

Left: Killer whales leave the Arctic waters in fall to pursue migrating salmon and some migrate to the south and west Irish coasts, including Cape Clear Island (County Cork). They often move in small family groups, preying on large fish as well as seals, porpoises, and dolphins.

Seals and seabirds

Other marine mammals include the Atlantic gray seal and the common seal, which look so appealing with their great dark round eyes. On shore the rugged coasts and cliffs are alive with nesting or visiting seabirds such as gannets, fulmars, enchanting clown-like puffins, and elegant black-and-white razorbills. Some of the world's largest breeding colonies gather here, while unusual migrants may include North American species unintentionally swept across the Atlantic by adverse weather on their long migration from Canada. Peregrine falcons haunt many of the coastal cliffs and rare corncrakes are found on the coastlines of Donegal and West Connaught.

Opposite: Between March and August, puffins nest in burrows or below rocky overhangs on steep cliffs in the Skelligs — a noisy nursery raucous with the cries of kittiwakes, guillemots, and gannets.

Below: Gray seals are powerful swimmers and are amazingly graceful and agile in the sea where they hunt fish. They have excellent vision with which to spot prey or they can use their sensitive whiskers to detect vibrations in murkier waters.

Below right: Peregrine falcons are supreme aerial hunters. They make spectacularly fast vertical dives as they plunge with outstretched razor-sharp talons — ready to strike other birds in mid-air.

Remarkable birds

The peregrine falcon *(Falco peregrinus)* is a most impressive and powerful falcon that dives in a vertical stoop to seize prey in mid-air, possibly topping speeds of up to 180mph (290kph) as it plummets to strike a prey bird with its outstretched razor-sharp talons. These bluish-gray raptors haunt coastal cliffs, mountain crags, quarries, moorland, marshes, and estuaries, often perching with hunched shoulders as their keen eyes scan the landscape — or flying with rapid wing-beats before a long glide. Peregrine numbers had fallen to dangerously low levels here until a 1970s pesticide ban gave them a fighting chance to recover. They lay their buff, red speckled eggs in nests and aeries on the rocky ledges of steep Irish cliffs.

Rare corncrakes

Another endangered species is the corncrake or land rail *(Crex crex)*. Once its rasping 'crex crex' call was a familiar sound, carrying for long distances on a still night, and being especially persistent if the bird was seeking a mate. Sadly, modern agricultural practices, such as mowing grass meadows, have devastated corncrake populations and it is virtually extinct in Ireland now, surviving in just a few special places like Tory Island in north Donegal, the Shannon Callows, west Mayo, and Rathlin Island off the coast of County Antrim. This highly secretive, gray, long-legged bird with rich chestnut wing panels is rarely seen as it hides among the long grass and vegetation of its favorite island haunts.

A circular tour

Just south of the border between Eire and Northern Ireland on the east coast is Dundalk, the county town of Louth, Ireland's smallest county. Its name derives from the prehistoric fort of Dún Dealgan that now bears a Norman motte, crowned by a castle folly raised in 1780 by a pirate. A little farther south Drogheda appears, a town founded by the Danes in 911 but soon becoming a Norman port that gained its charter as a town in 1194. This was the site of an infamous massacre by Oliver Cromwell's troops in 1649 following a prolonged siege. Later in 1690 the Battle of the Boyne's bitter fighting took place only some 4 miles (6km) west of the town. Long before all this turmoil, a burial mound had been constructed nearby at Newgrange in about 3200 BC — this is one of the best-preserved passage graves in Europe and is believed to be the world's most ancient solar observatory.

Above and below: More than 5000 years old, Newgrange passage grave is older than the Egyptian pyramids or Stonehenge. Its stones are decorated with spirals, circles, radials, lozenges, and chevrons.

Steep-cliffed, rugged Lambay is the largest island off the east coast of Ireland, situated a little north of Dublin. Here the RMS *Tayleur* (taking passengers to seek riches in Australia) was shipwrecked in 1854, with the loss of some 380 lives — just one of an estimated 12,000 or so recorded shipwrecks off the coast of Ireland since 1105. A Danish king of Dublin, Sitric, granted Lambay to Christ Church Cathedral and in 1181 Prince John presented it to the Dublin archbishops. Today Lambay is one of the most important seabird colonies in Ireland, with a population of over 50,000 common guillemots, 5000 kittiwakes, 3500 razorbills, 2500 pairs of herring gulls, and smaller numbers of puffins, Manx shearwaters, and fulmars. Ireland's only east-coast colony of gray seals lives here as well as a herd of fallow deer and, rather more surprisingly, wallabies — whose ancestors were exiled to the island in the 1980s when Dublin Zoo became overcrowded.

Howth Head

Just to the south, at the northern tip of Dublin Bay is Howth Head where a sturdy lighthouse braces itself against the buffeting winds. Just offshore is the bird sanctuary of Ireland's Eye, with a 19th-century Martello tower and the ruins of St Nessan's Church that date back to AD 700. Here is a renowned breeding colony of cormorants. Puffins nest and bob about too, fish trailing from their beaks, and on the massive freestanding Stack Rock hosts of seabirds (guillemots, razorbills, fulmars, and gulls) nest and squawk vociferously as gray seals peer out from the sea below.

Below: Once a fishing village, Howth is now a bustling Dublin suburb, set on a rugged peninsula. The lighthouse on Howth Head warns ships of the rugged rocks while walkers enjoy views of the sea, the Mountains of Mourne, and the lush Wicklow hills.

Left: There has been a lifeboat based at Howth harbor since 1817. The name 'Howth' derives from the Norse word hoved (meaning headland) — after the early Viking settlement here. Today a working fishing fleet, countless yachts, bobbing gray seals, and nearby seabird colonies compete for the attention of onlookers here.

Above: Large colonies of razorbills nest on coastal cliffs. At just over two weeks old, the single downy chick launches itself into the sea. Some tumble onto the rocks but they are protected by a thick layer of fat. These strong young swimmers will be fed by their parents out at sea until able to fly and fend for themselves.

Dublin and nearby

Dublin is an amazing city of great diversity — a former slave market, home to the Guinness brewing empire, Trinity College, the Book of Kells, and the very first MGM roaring lion, birthplace of Oscar Wilde, Jonathan Swift, and Bob Geldof, with many other fascinating attributes that will be explored fully in Chapter 3 (see pages 158–163).

Here the concentration is on its coastal location as a port used by the Vikings whose longships reached Ireland in 795. They founded Waterford, Limerick, and Dublin, sailing up the Liffey and ultimately establishing Dublin as a vital base, naval port, and trading center where the goods included slaves, especially Britons and Picts. Ships arrived carrying wine, ceramics, soapstone, silk from Baghdad, silver from the Middle East, and walrus tusks from the Arctic.

The original port was upriver at Wood Quay, close to Christ Church Cathedral. Dublin continued to be a bustling harbor through medieval times although wild and windy Dublin Bay was not always the most hospitable host and shipwrecks were common. Walls erected to protect the harbor include the North Bull Wall built at the recommendation of William Bligh in 1800 — he is better known as the stern captain who survived the mutiny on his ship, HMS *Bounty*.

Below: Dublin's neoclassical Custom House overlooks the River Liffey.

Opposite: East Pier lighthouse. In the 5th century King Laoghaire sent raiding ships to Britain and France from Dún Laoghaire.

A thriving port

In 1767, Poolbeg lighthouse was raised at the end of the South Bull Wall and by the 1800s it was luxury goods for the rich Georgian households that were regularly being shipped up the Liffey. Dublin continued to thrive and today it is Ireland's largest port where some 1.2 million ferry and cruise passengers arrive each year. The port and its land were recently valued at 25 to 30 billion Euros. As the port stretched farther downriver, the beautiful neoclassical Custom House, built in 1791, changed roles and became a government building instead. After attacks and a serious fire during the 1921 Irish War of Independence, it was restored and remains a beautiful and highly ornamental building adorned with sculpted heads that represent Ireland's rivers. It looks especially fine at night when floodlit in a golden glow.

Cockles and mussels

On the nearby seashores, countless clams, cockles, and mussels cling tenaciously to the rocks; they were famously collected by Miss Molly Malone to be sold on the Dublin streets. A statue to this celebrated fisherwoman who 'wheeled her wheelbarrow through streets broad and narrow' was erected on Grafton Street in Dublin in 1987. To the south of the city is Dublin's 'Riviera,' Dún Laoghaire, comprising a busy passenger ferry port, splendid harbor and yachting marina set against a backdrop of brightly painted houses, parks, and palm trees with rolling hills beyond. It is named for the High King Laoghaire who held court before the Vikings arrived.

Wicklow, Wexford, and Waterford

Wicklow, renowned for its lakes and beautiful mountains, is called the 'Garden of Ireland.' Heading south the first main town we encounter is Bray, which retains something of its Victorian resort origins and from whence the coast and railway wriggle south together past several popular shore fishing areas. Farther south is Wicklow itself, overlooking a wide bay and crescent-shaped curving coast. This was once an important Viking maritime base. Many centuries later it faced fierce repercussions after the 1798 Irish Rebellion against British rule had been supported by a good number of households here; many Wicklow men lost their lives or had to face transportation to the penal colony of New South Wales in Australia.

Previous pages: The iconic ESB Poolbeg chimneys on the edge of Dublin Bay have appeared in numerous photographs, but perhaps their most important cameo appearance came when they featured in the 'Pride (In the Name of Love)' music video by Irish rock band U2.

Opposite: Many people fish from Wicklow pier, hoping perhaps to catch coalfish, mackerel, dogfish, crabs, codling, or whiting.

Below: The Wicklow area hosts many fairs and festivals (including Bray Jazz in May). Bray's mile-long seafront encompasses a harbor, National Aquarium, and a Victorian promenade. Bray Head, the Sugar Loaf, and the Wicklow mountains rise behind.

Wexford

Continuing south, the stone and shingle beaches give way to golden sand. At Arklow, fish like bass, flounder, and codling are in plentiful supply and then, beyond Cahore Point, is Wexford, once long ago a major sea port, where ships arrived from all corners of the earth. It was named Waesfjord, the Norse word for an 'estuary with mud flats.' These still skirt its shores and are now a wildlife reserve for swans, waders, and white-fronted geese.

Just inland on the River Barrow, the *Dunbrody* at New Ross is a full-scale reproduction of a three-masted barque, a 19th-century famine ship that took a total of over two million Irish famine victims on their emigration voyages across the Atlantic. The museum commemorates some descendants of the fleeing Irish populace including the Kennedys, Henry Ford, and Commodore John Barry, who became a famous commander in the United States Navy.

Rosslare harbor is now southeast Ireland's main port, its star rising as the fortunes of the old Viking port in Wexford declined. It has a good stretch of beach and sand dunes. A little farther south, off the coast of Wexford, the lighthouse on Tuscar Rock marks a perilous navigational hazard that also witnessed an air disaster in 1968 — 61 people died when an Aer Lingus flight from Cork to London crashed into the sea. The birds and seals in evidence here now are oblivious both to the tragic accident and the breathtaking views.

Island sanctuary

Farther south, the two Saltee Islands off the southern coast of Wexford offer sanctuary to razorbills, puffins, guillemots, noisy gannets — spectacular divers that plunge at high speed into the sea — and cormorants that dive from the surface of the water to snatch up fish and eels. A colony of gray seals lives here too, catching fish and crustaceans expertly (and the occasional squid and octopus).

Hook Head and Waterford harbor

One of Europe's oldest lighthouses is set at Hook Head on Ireland's south coast, guarding the entrance to Waterford harbor and close to the site of a 5th-century monastery. For over 700 years the monks kept a warning beacon burning here. Opposite Hook Head is the village of Crooke — and Oliver Cromwell's 1649 threat to take Waterford 'by hook or by crook' may have given rise to this popular saying.

Founded by Vikings in AD 914, Waterford — famous for its crystal-glass factory — is Ireland's oldest city. Reginald's Tower, an Anglo-Norman stone structure, marks the site of the Viking fort. Waterford became a major seaport and fishing boats still gather at Passage East and Dunmore East below cliffs busy with kittiwakes.

Dungarvan

Named for Saint Garbhan, who founded a monastery here in the 600s, Dungarvan is the county town of Waterford. It is a busy port and market town set at the mouth of the Colligan river with its harbor almost entirely encircled by the sand spit and curving bay, its waters fed by several small rivers and streams. The English King John raised the castle by the harbor in about 1200. The majestic Comeragh mountains rise behind miles of sandy beaches, mudflats, and saltmarshes that bustle with thousands of waders and wildfowl, including pintails and shovelers, gulls, brent geese, grebes, skuas, gannets, terns, egrets, godwits, redshanks, and oystercatchers. Conveniently for them, there are oyster farms too!

Opposite: Hook Head lighthouse is one of the world's oldest working lighthouses, having warned ships off the rocks for over seven centuries. Earlier a 5th-century beacon was tended by monks.

Below: Dunmore East is a popular tourist and fishing village with a picturesque sheltered harbor.

Below left: Nesting gannets mate for life, their reunions marked by elaborate greeting rituals as they gently tap their bills together.

County Cork

Dropping south of the walled town and fishing port of Youghal, granted to Sir Walter Raleigh by Elizabeth I, is Cobh, set on Great Island in Cork harbor and once called Queenstown. This was a major port for merchant ships and some claim that Cork is the world's second largest natural harbor. From here many Irish emigrants left to seek a new life in the Americas, taking their families across the Atlantic from the late 1700s onward. In the 1830s, almost 400,000 Irish left for North America and in 1847, when the Great Famine was wracking Ireland, the number of Irish immigrants to the United States reached 118,120 in that one year alone. However, this was a continuing flow and between 1848 and 1950 some 2.5 million Irish people emigrated to America and Canada from Cobh making it the single most important port of emigration in Ireland. Other ships set sail with cargoes of convicts bound for Australia's penal colony: 40,000 were despatched in the so-called 'coffin ships' from 1791 to 1853. Here too was where the RMS *Titanic* made her last port of call before setting off toward her devastating collision with an iceberg in April 1912 that cost some 1512 lives.

Above: Poverty, dire famine, and a desperate need for survival or (in later years) opportunity spearheaded a mass exodus from Ireland. As well as being Ireland's main emigration port, Cobh was also a major disembarkation center for men, women, and children who were deported to penal colonies, such as those in Australia.

Right: In Cobh, steep streets scramble up toward the cathedral set high above the busy waterfront. Because of its naturally protected harbor Cobh has historically been important as a tactical station for nautical military operations and became a British naval base during the Napoleonic wars between France and England.

Left: Smooth-sided sandstone pillars of the impressive Drombeg circle perch on a rocky terrace with the sea glinting in the distance. A high portal stone rises opposite a long recumbent — the midpoint of which has a conspicuous notch set in line with distant hills to provide a view of the winter solstice sunset. 1950s excavations near the circle's center revealed cremated bones in a deliberately broken pot wrapped with cloth.

Below: Pretty Kinsale harbor on the estuary of the Bandon River; the Lusitania sank just 8 miles (13km) off the Old Head of Kinsale. Many of the 1198 victims were buried at the Church of St Multose in Kinsale or in Queenstown (now called Cobh).

Kinsale

Just a little farther south, Kinsale nestles between the hills and the shoreline, with dolphin and whale-watching trips on offer from a harbor guarded by the 17th-century star-shaped bastion of Charles Fort. The Old Head of Kinsale has magnificent cliff scenery. In 1915 this area witnessed the sinking of the RMS *Lusitania* with a loss of nearly 1200 lives when the passenger liner was torpedoed by a German submarine; many of the victims are buried in the old church cemetery here.

The Druid's Altar

West of Clonakilty is the Drombeg stone circle, called the Druid's Altar and dating back to around 945-830 BC. It is set on the edge of a rocky terrace with fine views across to the sea. Close to this circle of great stones are the remains of two stone prehistoric dwellings and a Stone Age cooking trough in which water was probably boiled by dropping red-hot stones into the pit in order to cook a hearty meal of venison perhaps.

Baltimore

In 1631 a hundred citizens from nearby Baltimore were seized by Algerian pirates and forced into slavery, taken far away from their homeland. The place names hereabouts are wonderfully evocative — Roaringwater Bay, Carbery's Hundred Isles and dramatic Cape Clear on Clear Island with its lighthouse and observatory. This is a good place to see guillemots, storm petrels, fulmars, kittiwakes, skuas, cormorants, and sooty and great shearwaters, as well as Manx shearwaters *(Puffinus puffinus)*. These birds have been known to reach 55 years of age and one record-breaker is calculated to have flown around 5 million miles (8 million km) during its lifetime. They nest in burrows, usually emerging at night to hunt so as to avoid being hunted themselves. In winter, they migrate some 6200 miles (10,000km) to waters off the coasts of Brazil and Argentina in South America. Basking sharks, seals, dolphins, and, sometimes, whales can be spotted in these waters too.

The harbor at Schull (or Skull) is popular with visiting yachtsmen. Mount Gabriel rises above, topped by giant golf-ball-like radar domes that track aircraft as they travel out over the Atlantic. On its slopes are the remains of a Bronze Age copper mine where spearheads, axes, and intricately fashioned ornaments have been found. The peninsula leads on to Mizen Head, the southwestern tip of Ireland where fierce rocky cliffs — here and there softened by wild flowers — confront swirling Atlantic Ocean tides. A major north-south bird migration flight path lies just a mile offshore and close by is the Fastnet Rock Lighthouse — the last landfall seen by many Irish emigrants to America and the site of one of Guglielmo Marconi's first electric telegraph stations.

Bantry Bay

Bantry Bay is a large, deep natural harbor a little to the north with a very long inlet, the sea hemmed in by high mountain ridges down which silver streams cascade. French fleets arrived here in 1689 to support James II against William of Orange — and again in 1796 to help Wolfe Tone and the Irish uprising. On that occasion the vessels were dispersed by a fierce storm so only a few ships reached the bay.

Island garden

Close to Bantry is Glengariff and Garnish Island (also known as Ilnacullin), a fascinating island garden where the sheltered situation and warming Gulf Stream encourage the growth of lush subtropical flowers in classical, Italian, and Japanese-style gardens. This area of west Ireland remains remote. Banks of fuchsia and rhododendrons glow against the ragged limestone and slate cliffs dotted with wild flowers. The daunting Beara peninsula was once the haunt of smugglers landing contraband like French brandy. Perhaps they were observed by the vigilant birds perched on the ruined castle on Dursey Island that is reached via Ireland's only cable car. It is licensed to transport just three passengers and one cow!

The deeply indented coast, scattered with old cottages, stone circles, and ancient abandoned mines, twists past Crow Head and stretches northward into Kerry and then all along the western edge of Ireland.

Left: The natural harbor of Bantry Bay, with the Beara peninsula beyond, dotted with fishing villages — once a haven for smugglers.

Opposite: The high cliffs of Mizen Head face swirling Atlantic waves; the haunt of dolphins, whales, seals, gannets, and kittiwakes.

County Kerry
Kenmare and the Ring of Kerry

Kenmare, set on the deep estuary of the river that shares its name, lies between the rugged Ring of Beara and the renowned Ring of Kerry that follows the coastline of the Iveragh peninsula. It is famous for its traditional lace, once made by the local women who were taught these skills by nuns from St Clare's Convent when they desperately needed extra income during the famine years. Even farther back in the mists of time, druids gathered to make human sacrifices at the ancient stone circle here. Celtic finds include axes and a dagger that date back to 1800-2000 BC, but Kerry's mountainous finger of land, jutting out into the Atlantic Ocean, is sprinkled with over 2000 ancient monuments. Pillar stones, standing stones, circles, and ring forts mark the older beliefs but these were superseded when Christianity reached the southwest of Ireland relatively early, even before Saint Patrick so famously spread the word.

The Ring of Kerry follows the coastline of the mountainous Iveragh peninsula and many visitors take this 109-mile (175km) dramatic scenic drive past picturesque villages and many beautiful sandy coves that are so evocative of Ireland's special atmosphere that has inspired countless artists, authors, and cinema directors. David Lean's 1970 classic *Ryan's Daughter* was filmed here.

Below: The enchanting indented coastline of Kerry where even the name has a fine, appealing ring to it!

The Skelligs

Out at sea are the Skelligs, rocky islands rising sharply from the sea that are famous for their superb seabird colonies and magnificent scenery. Beehive cells and boat-shaped oratories are also found here where 6th-century monks once created religious manuscripts in this wild setting or carved the 600 stone steps that scramble up the steep rock face of Skellig Michael. Depending on the time of year, this is a good place to see seals and their pups, basking sharks, turtles, and dolphins. Guillemots, razorbills, and fulmars nest here as do Atlantic puffins *(Fratercula arctica)*, flaunting their huge bills, which are brightly colored in the breeding season. They breed in large colonies on coastal cliffs or offshore islands, nesting in rock crevices or in burrows in the soil. Their short wings whirr rapidly, beating up to 100 times per minute as they fly low over the ocean, ready to dive for fish when they virtually fly under the water in pursuit of their prey. They can dive to depths of around 230ft (70m).

Amazing birds

Storm petrels, Europe's smallest seabirds, were named for Saint Peter because they sometimes appear to walk across the water; the 'storm' element of the name refers to their habit of often seeking shelter in the lee of ships during fierce weather. One famous Skellig resident was a petrel included in the *Guinness Book of Records* on account of her regular winter vacations in the balmier regions of South Africa. 'Stormy' made this annual return flight of 12,400 miles (20,000km) for at least 26 years.

On pyramid-shaped Small Skellig some 23,000 pairs of gannets crowd onto every available crack or ledge, while seals relax on the lower rocks, sometimes slithering off to drop into the water if disturbed by a passing boat.

Fossilized footprints

From Portmagee a causeway leads to Valentia Island where huge Atlantic swells smash powerfully against the rocks. There are fossilized footprints here, made by a tetrapod (a salamander-type creature) some 385 million years ago and preserved in the Devonian Age mud — the oldest such trackway ever found in the northern hemisphere. For a century, transatlantic telegraph cables were transmitted from this island as it was the eastern terminal of a transatlantic telegraph cable service. The service was suspended in 1966. Today this is the setting for Glanleam House; this is now a hotel and its subtropical gardens contain a glorious profusion of rare and tender plants.

Cahirciveen is a small rural market town and the capital of the Iveragh peninsula at the foot of Benetee mountain overlooking Valentia harbor. Daniel O'Connell — a prominent Irish political leader in the 19th century — was born here. The heritage center is set in a cone-shaped tower once used by the British as a lookout. A little farther north stands Glenbeigh, a tiny fishing village with a long beach. Mud flats offer good bird watching and the Kerry Bog Village features reconstructed thatched cottages dating from the 1800s including a blacksmith's forge, a turfcutter's house, a stable dwelling, and a dairy.

Above: *The magnificent Skellig Islands rise majestically from the sea, with awe-inspiring rock formations, a 6th-century monastic settlement and an impressive colony of some 23,000 pairs of nesting gannets.*

Left: *The beehive-shaped clocháns on Skellig Michael are perched above perilously steep cliffs. For six centuries the monastery was an important center, having survived several Viking raids.*

County Kerry: the Dingle peninsula

The Dingle peninsula, pinpricked with wild red fuchsias, is the next major outcrop of land that thrusts into the Atlantic with the Ring of Kerry scenic route at its tip. At Annascaul, the blue-and-white South Pole Inn was built by Tom Crean, the Antarctic explorer who sailed with Ernest Shackleton in the small lifeboat on the rescue voyage from Elephant Island to South Georgia when the *Endurance* was crushed in ice. Next is pretty little Dingle, one of the most westerly towns in mainland Europe. One of the harbor's most famous residents is a male bottlenose dolphin called Fungie who, from 1984, has accompanied fishing boats and has swum with the visitors. Dingle's Oceanworld Aquarium offers a further opportunity to become better acquainted with the local sea creatures.

Horse races used to be held on the beach by Ventry village. Meanwhile legends tell how warrior Fionn Mac Cumhail (Finn McCool) defeated several kings here. Beyond is the Iron Age Dunbeg promontory fort and ancient beehive huts (clocháns) set on the tip of the peninsula near the scenic coastal ring road. While usually serving as places for monastic meditation, here they were evidently a cluster of dwellings and were later used for storage or animal shelters.

Looking west

Slea Head marks the southwestern end of the Dingle peninsula. Beyond lie the mountainous Blasket Islands that look idyllic when the sea is blue and calm (one is called the sleeping giant) but they can be treacherous too. A number of the Spanish Armada ships were wrecked here. A little farther north and just inland is the Gallarus Oratory — a tiny drystone church built between the 6th and the 9th century, just 10 by 15ft (3 by 4.5m) in size and shaped like an upturned boat.

Close to Tralee, the county town of Kerry, is Blennerville windmill, built in 1800, and a restored narrow gauge steam railway that runs from Blennerville to Ballyard and Tralee. The romantic ruins of Ardfert cathedral and the Franciscan friary merit a visit before leaving Kerry, as does the ruined keep of Carrigafoyle castle, raised in the 1490s but savaged by Cromwell's forces in 1649.

Below: Many artists try to capture the magic of Dingle's sheltered harbor with its fine new marina, bobbing boats, and regular visits by Fungie the dolphin. Overlooking the harbor is an excellent aquarium and sea-life center where the amazing underwater world of the Atlantic is revealed to interested visitors.

Following pages: Rocky Clogher Head beach on the Dingle peninsula; dusk descends brushing both cloud-tossed sky and tidal ripples with a soft pink glow.

Left: The Gallarus Oratory, believed to be an early Christian church, is a boat-shaped stone building. Its thick walls were constructed without mortar. Despite exposure to the wild Atlantic gales and lashing rain for over 1200 years it remains waterproof and is a masterpiece of fine stonework.

Below: This whitewashed cottage and ancient beehive dwelling are on mountainous Great Blasket Island, situated 3 miles (4.8km) off the tip of Dingle peninsula. In 1588 several Spanish Armada ships were wrecked on rocks nearby. Today breeding seabirds include guillemots, cormorants, kittiwakes, razorbills, puffins, shags, fulmars, Manx shearwaters, and storm petrels.

County Clare and the Cliffs of Moher

Beyond Kerry Head and the mouth of the River Shannon lies County Clare. During the Great Hunger, unsympathetic landlords evicted many tenants from lands here. Perhaps they took heart from the views of the ocean with America far beyond, holding the promise of a new and better life. At Loop Head, with its lighthouse set above the wild coastline, the Atlantic crashes against dizzyingly sheer cliffs where the hungry waves have, over the centuries, carved out sweeping slabs and huge caves below beetling overhangs. Mal Bay is named for Mal, a witch or enchantress who is reputed in local folklore to have chased the hero Cúchulainn south to Loop Head but drowned when trying to match his long-jumping skills. Her body was washed ashore at Mal Bay.

Just north, at Hag's Head, the justifiably renowned Cliffs of Moher appear — they attract a million visitors each year. They rise 702ft (214m) at their highest point above the ocean and stretch nearly 5 miles (8km) along the western seaboard with O'Brien's Tower set at (about) the halfway point. Majestic and awe-inspiring, they have been sculpted by the sea into vast towering blocks, russet red at sunset, whose stern faces offer some respite from the winds and dashing seaspray to colonies of seabirds that crouch on their ledges or seek cover in the grassland and heath atop the mighty cliffs. The 30,000 birds here (and on nearby Goat Island) include guillemots, puffins, gulls, shags, hawks, ravens, and choughs.

Above and right: The mighty Cliffs of Moher take their name from a ruined promontory fort, Mothar. They are one of the most impressive places to see in Ireland, and are widely considered to be the country's top tourist attraction. The cliffs are featured in the opening sequences of David Lean's 1970 movie Ryan's Daughter.

The Burren

A little farther north, lying just inland from the coast is the Burren, a barren limestone region formed some 350 million years ago where the contorted rocks and hillocks are home to amazing wildflowers and many ancient burial sites (see also page 90). Poulnabrone Dolmen, a Neolithic portal tomb, is among the most famous landmarks in the Burren and is estimated as being 4500 years old. During an archeological excavation at Poulnabrone the remains of more than 20 adults and children were found, together with a polished stone ax, some bone and flint items, and broken pieces of pottery.

Above: The Burren is a barren limestone karst landscape that hosts some superb wildflower specimens (including startling blue gentians) and many ancient archeological sites. The limestone cliffs and caves here are popular with rock climbers and potholers.

Right: Poulnabrone is just one of more than 70 megalithic tombs in the Burren. It seems to have been an important ceremonial site where people of some standing were interred; radiocarbon dating suggests that these burials occurred between about 3800 and 3200 BC.

Galway and Mayo

Galway flourished as a trading post in medieval times. It was a walled city controlled by 14 merchant families from 1396, declining in status only after the Battle of the Boyne in 1690, which ensured that the Williamite factions fighting in Ireland gained the upper hand over the Jacobites that Galway supported. It is famous for its old quays and wooden sailing boats called Galway hookers. The coastline that sweeps west and then north is home to many fishing villages and shores that are busy with oystercatchers, teals, curlews — and even scuba divers!

The waters from Galway Bay stretch out to encircle the three Aran Islands that host a plethora of prehistoric forts, monastic settlements, and ancient churches. Inishmore, the largest island, is home to the incredible 2500-year-old Bronze Age fort of Dun Aonghasa, its massive curved stone walls perched on the edge of a towering cliff that plummets a dizzying 330ft (100m) into the Atlantic Ocean below.

Several peninsulas thrust out into the ocean from Galway's fringe while Connemara, a wild area in the western extremes of Galway, offers the visitor coastal bogs, mountains, megalithic tombs, standing stones, and a rugged coastline. Just south of Clifden is the site of the original Marconi long-wave wireless station where transmissions were beamed to Nova Scotia. Here too pioneer aviators Alcock and Brown arrived after the historic first non-stop transatlantic flight from Newfoundland in 1919, crashlanding in Derrygimlagh bog.

The coast stretches on in a chain of bays, inlets, creeks, islands, and headlands, past mist-swathed Inishbofin island with its beautiful beaches and wild flowers, blowholes, fine sea stacks, seal colonies, and birds that include corncrakes, common and Arctic terns, many types of gull, fulmars, shags, guillemots, Manx shearwaters and choughs. Next comes Killary Head and harbor — and then County Mayo. Here, set in Clew Bay, is Clare Island — dotted with Iron Age sites, and once the base for the pirate queen and Irish patriot Grace O'Malley, a seafarer, trader, and clan chieftain in the 16th century who at one point was reprieved from hanging just as the noose was placed around her neck. She won the admiration of Elizabeth I and the English court for her bravado and wit.

Opposite: Oscar Wilde accurately described the landscape of Connemara as having a 'savage beauty.'

Below: The long coastal rim of Galway is indented by numerous harbors, deep landlocked bays, and countless small loughs that slice across the western mountains. This rocky shore stretches across to the Twelve Pins — a range of sharp-peaked quartzite hills.

Opposite: The impressive limestone cliffs at Dun Aonghasa (or Dun Aengus) on Inishmore; a beautiful wild island with crumbling stone walls, swooping birds, and ancient prehistoric forts teetering at the edge of sheer cliffs. This is one of the finest prehistoric sites in Western Europe.

Right: Dun Duchatair (Black Fort) is an Iron Age stone promontory fort that now encompasses the remains of beehive huts. It is set high on the cliffs of Inishmore, the largest Aran Island.

Below: Aran is the place to buy fine Aran sweaters and hats, Celtic jewelry or Irish drums (bodhrans) in between bracing walks to absorb the magical seascapes and views of Inisheer's 1857 lighthouse.

Soon Ireland's biggest island looms into view, the mainly boggy Achill that is joined to the mainland by a road bridge. The landscape here is dominated by Slievemore mountain. Sharks are sometimes spotted off Keem Bay.

On the mainland, just north of Achill, the Mullet peninsula projects over Blacksod Bay where there are mudflats, sandflats, and saltmarshes. Off to the west lie several islands including Inis Glora — associated with Saint Brendan the Navigator, an early monastic saint who, in the early 500s, supposedly sailed across the Atlantic to Newfoundland in a leather boat (a voyage re-enacted in 1976 by explorer Tim Severin). In Irish legend the fabled four children of Lir, doomed to wander Ireland for nine centuries as enchanted singing swans, spent their last three centuries here before finally becoming human once more — and promptly withering to dust.

Stone Age enclosure

The northern boundary of North Mayo is exposed to the wild Atlantic that pummels the 600-million-year old rocks of the Stags of Broadhaven. The cliffs at Céide, Ballycastle, reach a height of 365ft (111m). Céide Fields is Europe's biggest Stone Age land enclosure; here, some 5000 years ago, 4sq miles (10km²) of fields were enclosed by walls so that crops could grow and cattle safely graze. Fields, houses, and megalithic tombs were preserved beneath the bogland. They were discovered only in the 1930s, long hidden under a thick springy mantle of peat, mosses, lichens, sedges, and countless moisture-loving flowers.

Nearby, at Downpatrick Head, a plaque commemorates those who lost their lives in the wake of the 1798 Irish rebellion. This is a formidable landscape: the Atlantic has gouged a huge bay from the massive cliffs that are populated with high and cavernous blowholes that spew out sea spray. Such remarkable scenery is said to have been created when Saint Patrick was fighting the Devil (or a king who refused to be converted) and struck such a powerful blow with his crosier that part of the headland broke away. This lone stack of rock, now crowned by a crumbling fort, is a mass of nesting fulmars, guillemots, and kittiwakes while in the skies above peregrines, ravens, and choughs also fly — as migrating whales surge though the ocean below. Killala Bay, equally bustling with birdlife, opens up the portal to the next county — Sligo.

Opposite: Achill's rugged coastal routes offer unrivaled solitude.

Below: The summit of misty Croagh Patrick was long ago a sacred pagan site. Now a little church at the top attracts Christian pilgrims. Saint Patrick visited in AD 441 and, from the mountain peak, legend records that he banished dragons, snakes, and demons.

Below left: A ruined castle tower on Achill island, a place where beautiful flowers and grasses flourish on peatland and bog.

Sligo, Leitrim, and Donegal

Sligo was the boyhood home of poet W.B. Yeats. He is buried at Drumcliff churchyard here and spent many summers at Rosses Point at the entrance to Sligo Bay. Out at sea is Inishmurray, a holy island, long ago a place of pilgrimage and the site of a monastic settlement. Here barnacle geese prepare for their annual migratory return flight to Greenland.

Leitrim only just nudges the sea, the briefest shoreline of any Irish coastal county measuring a scant 2 miles (3km) before Bundoran introduces the deeply indented coast of Donegal that wriggles on ahead past Killybegs, where they make carpets and tapestries but which is best known as a fishing port. Iceland, glaucous, and herring gulls follow the busy trawlers and every summer Killybegs hosts a street festival to celebrate the catches (usually mackerel and herring) and to stage the traditional ceremony of the Blessing of the Boats.

Opposite: At Donega's Slieve League, the cliffs rise precipitously above the raging ocean with magnificent views all around.

Below: Stunning coastal vistas, castles, and beaches draw visitors to Glencolumbkille (Valley of Saint Columba).

Around Donegal

Donegal Bay is Ireland's largest bay and home to one of the highest sea cliffs in Europe, which rises a sheer breathtaking 1972ft (601m) at Slieve League, with a dizzying walk along knife-edged One Man's Path offering dramatic views to those brave enough to tackle it.

Beyond lie the many beautiful windswept beaches and sandy coves that abound in Donegal, made the more romantic by low purple mountains rising behind. The scenery here has aroused the enthusiasm of 20th-century playwright and poet Frank McGuinness, contemporary playwright and local resident Brian Friel who has set many of his plays in Donegal, and Irish poet William Allingham (1824–1889).

Tradition has it that Saint Columba (521–597) was born in Donegal; he played a major part in the development of the Church in Ireland, Scotland, and northern England. The Glencolumbkille coastline is named for him, it being a dramatic mix of sheer cliffs, sandy beaches, sea-sculpted rocks, and tiny inlets where local fishermen moor their boats. Before Columba's time the circular earth and stoneworks were raised during the Celtic period above the Silver Strand at Malinbeg and on the Doonalt promontory.

From Ardara, Donegal's weaving capital, the coast wriggles and squiggles north to the rocky headland of the Rosses, sprinkled with over a hundred lakes, while out at sea, Arranmore Island looms 750ft (228m) high — Ireland's second largest island is home to over 600 people. The coast sweeps on regardless of their busy lives, past other islands sprinkled liberally here, to reach Bloody Foreland — so called because of how its rocks glow crimson at sunset. Tory Island lies out at sea to the north and bears a round tower and ruined monastery, founded in the 6th century by Saint Columba. Back on the mainland, a lofty rock rises precipitously over the sea at Sheephaven Bay; this is Horn Head where there are many Neolithic tombs and stone circles, as well as Napoleonic and World War II lookout towers, derelict Horn Head House, a dramatic blowhole called McSwyne's Gun, towering cliffs and, as ever, a cacophony of noisy seabirds including razorbills and European shags.

Left: Falcarragh (Donegal) is situated on a narrow inlet. Some 6000 years ago Mesolithic hunters from Scotland paddled into Ballyness Bay and settled here.

Opposite below: Balor, the legendary king of Tory Island, was a giant. Today the island is buffeted by gigantic Atlantic seas and storms as 36ft (11m) waves lash the 100ft (30m) high cliffs behind West Town.

Below: Malin Head, Ireland's most northerly point, boasts some of Europe's biggest sand dunes. From here it is possible to see Scotland on a clear day and spot a wide range of birds including corncrakes, gannets, shearwaters, skuas, and auks.

Hell's Hole

The Inishowen peninsula encompasses rugged Malin Head, Ireland's most northerly point (except for the small rocky island of Inishtrahull). The dramatic cliffs overlook a sea-churning chasm called Hell's Hole and house a cliff-face hermit's cave — the Wee House of Malin. Here too is the fishing port of Greencastle, named for the romantic, ruined greenstone castle, now emerald with scrambling plants instead. The wonderfully named Lough Swilly is a narrow fjord-like Atlantic Ocean inlet, overlooked by Dunree Fort, which has been standing guard ever since a time of potential invasion by the French in the Napoleonic era. At Grianan Ailigh the imposing circular stone ramparts were possibly a pagan temple some 2500 years ago but became the palace of the O'Neills from AD 450. This wild peninsula provides a suitably dramatic finale as now borders are crossed and Northern Ireland awaits.

Into Northern Ireland

In 1921, the province of Northern Ireland was created when the island of Ireland was partitioned. For many years since it has been associated with Ireland's turbulent political times. Now, with recent political agreements leading toward a lasting peace and reconciliation, once again the area draws eager visitors — who find much to see and enjoy here.

The estuary mudflats at Lough Foyle near Londonderry are home to flocks of visiting brent geese and whooper swans while at its eastern tip lies the 6 mile (10km) expanse of Benone Strand, Ireland's longest beach with Magilligan Point at its western end crowned by a Martello tower that was built in 1812. There are wonderful sand dunes here, with many flowers in both meadows and dunes that throng with butterflies, moths, and bees. A few miles farther on is Mussenden temple,

a domed basalt and sandstone rotunda built in 1785 on a clifftop ledge, ostensibly to serve as a library for the Bishop of Derry but rumors suggest it was actually a place where he might enjoy liaisons with his mistress.

From Giant's Causeway to Carrickfergus

The coast leads on past the rather creepy ruins of Dunluce Castle to one of Ireland's most famous and spectacular sights: the Giant's Causeway in County Antrim, a National Nature Reserve and Northern Ireland's only World Heritage Site. Its mass of some 40,000 basalt columns — made by the crystallization of cooling lava some 60 million years ago — seem to march inexorably into the sea. They were described by poet William Thackeray as a 'remnant of chaos.' A few of the columns have four, five, seven, or eight sides but most are

hexagonal, with some of the taller examples looming up a towering 40ft or so (12m).

Finn McCool

Once folk believed this was the work of the legendary giant Finn McCool, a warrior and commander of the king's armies who built it as a route to reach a female giant with whom he was enamored; she lived on Staffa, a Hebrides island where there is a Scottish equivalent of this basalt rock formation. Others claim that two giants were arguing across the waters separating Ireland from Scotland. Finn McCool created the causeway to Scotland so that they could fight. Tired from his labors, Finn McCool pretended to be a baby asleep in his cot. His adversary, Benandonner, was tricked into believing that if this baby was so huge, the full-grown giant must be absolutely enormous so he ran back across the sea to Scotland, tearing up the causeway as he went. The tops of the columns certainly do resemble stepping stones leading into the sea and there are many contorted formations which have been given colorful names, such as the Giant's Granny, Honeycomb, Wishing Well and the King and his Nobles.

Above: Lonely Dunluce Castle was once surrounded by a bustling merchant village, but this was burned in 1641 when an Irish army besieged the castle during the rebellion.

Following pages: The Giant's Causeway (called the Eighth Wonder of the World in the 18th century) has witnessed many shipwrecks over the centuries. When the Spanish Armada's Girona sank in 1588, some 1200 unfortunate sailors drowned in these waters.

A Spanish Armada ship *Girona* foundered at Port na Spaniagh near the Giant's Causeway in 1588 with the loss of more than 1200 men; its mighty cannons found a home in nearby St Cuthbert's graveyard and in 1967 treasure hunters discovered ducats, muskets, jeweled chains, and golden cameos. Fierce storms sank almost 30 of the Spanish Armada ships off the coast of Ireland and many sailors were drowned and much booty looted by the local chieftains. Today the area is a haven for birds — razorbills, cormorants, fulmars, petrels, redshanks, guillemots, choughs, and peregrine falcons — as well as plants like sea spleenwort, frog orchid, hare's foot trefoil, vernal squill, sea fescue — and lots of kelp.

Dotted around the coast are farms, sheltered harbors, slipways, and fishermen's cottages. Between the mainland and a small island used by salmon fishermen, the Carrick-a-Rede rope bridge spans its swinging vertiginous way across an awesome 80ft (24m) chasm.

First wireless message

Scotland is only a stone's throw away now with Torr Head a mere 13 miles (21km) from the Mull of Kintyre. Ballycastle harbor has a memorial commemorating the work of Guglielmo Marconi and the first wireless message that was sent to Rathlin Island in 1898. This is a treeless arc-shaped spot just over 6 miles (9km) offshore where the Vikings first raided Ireland in 795. In 1575 the English perpetrated an infamous massacre (one of the leaders was Francis Drake), killing hundreds of women and children seeking refuge there. Today it is more peaceful, except for the buffeting winds and the calls of thousands of seabirds around its 230ft (70m) high cliffs. The lighthouse is unusual — appearing almost 'upside down' with the beacon at the bottom of the tower instead of the top and flashing red instead of yellow. Here too is Bruce's Cave where the Scottish king was reputedly inspired by the perseverance of the patient spider remaking her web. He arrived with his troops at Larne in 1315 — a popular landing place since Mesolithic times, a busy seaport for over 1000 years, and another port from which many Irish emigrants sailed to seek a new life in America.

Next is the peninsula of Islandmagee for which, in Elizabethan times, the Bissett family paid their annual rent in the form of goshawks that bred on the chalky cliffs. Here too is the (at least) 4000-year-old Ballylumford dolmen (another one popularly called Druid's Altar) with its mighty capstone. Beyond, set on a low stone crag overlooking the harbor and in a position that commanded Belfast Lough, lies the splendid Norman castle of Carrickfergus, built between the 1180s and 1250, which is complete with its original portcullis.

Opposite: Carrick-a-Rede rope bridge was built by salmon fishermen — some visitors cannot face the return walk across the swaying bridge and have to be taken off the island by boat.

Above: Waves sweep to shore at Ballycastle, County Antrim. In the 15th century the harbor here was known as Port Brittas and later it became the main port for coal boats from mines at nearby Fair Head.

Belfast and beyond

Belfast (from the Irish Béal Feirste meaning the sandy ford at the River Farset's mouth) became the capital of Northern Ireland in 1920. More can be discovered about the city on pages 134–137. Suffice to say here that this is a fine, and very ancient place: the Giant's Ring is a 5000-year-old site near the city and the remains of many Iron Age hill forts dot the surrounding hills. One of them, Cavehill, was said to have been the inspiration for Swift's recumbent giant in *Gulliver's Travels* when the author was residing at Lilliput Cottage in Belfast. Occupied since the Bronze Age, Belfast is famous for its linen, ropemaking, tobacco works, and shipbuilding — including the ill-fated liner the *Titanic*. The engineer who designed her, Thomas Andrews, lost his life on board — after directing many others to safety.

To the east and pointing south like a bent finger lies the Ards peninsula and the Copeland islands where only seabirds live. Ballycopeland boasts County Down's only working windmill while across the peninsula is the Scrabo country park and a rather dainty pinnacled tower memorial overlooking the shore. To the south and just inland is Downpatrick, named for the Irish patron saint, reputedly buried here in 461. Stories tell how Saint Patrick was kidnapped by pirates in Britain and brought to Ireland where he ultimately spread the Christian faith. He was also said to have banished all the snakes here, driving them into the sea. Certainly Ireland is indeed free of these reptiles but perhaps (more prosaically) because when snakes spread from the supercontinent Gondwanaland, Ireland was still completely underwater. Even the vast Cliffs of Moher were merely chalky sediments accumulating on the seabed.

Now the coastline gently crinkles its way south and eventually, as the famous song says, 'the mountains of Mourne sweep down to the sea.' Here moody purple mountains and emerald foothills — so typical of Ireland's scenery — rise behind castles and fishing villages and the wave-tossed coastal rim. Southern Ireland waits ahead once more and our 3500-mile (5600km) coastal circuit is complete.

Opposite: Downpatrick Head. Having gouged a huge bay from the mighty cliffs, the Atlantic (or legends say Saint Patrick) separated off a towering stack of rock where wheeling birds now circle the column.

Below: A lighthouse at the seaside resort of Newcastle where the beautiful Mountains of Mourne sweep down almost to the beach.

Chapter 2

THE IRISH LANDSCAPE

This is a place of infinite variety — of moody moors and haunted peat bogs, purple mountain peaks, steep rocky chasms, lush emerald valleys, and field and farmland where cottages offer warm comfort on those bitter winter nights when the wind blows cold. There are wide rivers, bubbling streams, and gushing waterfalls. Often soft falling rain dimples the surface of a magically shimmering lake. History has imprinted its mark on the landscape too — with ancient dolmens, standing stones, prehistoric circles, and the silhouettes of Celtic crosses and sturdy castles bearing witness to Ireland's rich cultural heritage.

Above: Peaceful Lough Derryclare in Connemara, County Galway.

Left: Annascaul on the Dingle peninsula — a paradise for walkers.

Ireland is blessed with a wealth of different rural landscapes — like an artist's palette which contributes glorious green and purple splashes for the land, blue-washed cloud-tossed skies and bright dabs of golden gorse, corn, or bracken. The coastline zigzags around Ireland's kidney-shaped outline, enclosing a pastoral scene long vanished from more heavily industrialized nations. Here most of the cities or busy towns cling to the coastal fringes or river estuaries while a great central plain, bounded by hills and mountains, flows inland from the eastern coastal fringe.

The rural scene

Ireland can boast high moors and low-lying marshes, moody peat bogs, a patchwork of fields and farmland, rugged high peaks, wide valleys, and steep chasms. There are broad rivers, rushing streams, almost a thousand shimmering lakes and everywhere, standing witness to life in ancient times, are to be found dolmens, standing stones, and prehistoric circles that rise as silent pointers to Ireland's rich past — as do the dramatic Celtic crosses that were erected all over Christian Ireland from the 7th to the 12th centuries.

Above: Ancient Celtic crosses like this lichen-encrusted example are to be found in countless Irish churchyards.

Right: A cloud-tossed sky and slender reeds are reflected in the peat-stained water of this tranquil Connemara lake.

Ireland's wildlife: an overview

After the last Ice Age, Ireland was separated from the European mainland by water and so it has a rather more restricted range of flora and fauna than may be found elsewhere in Europe. However, as if to compensate for this, many species have survived and flourished well in this geographically isolated haven.

Wetlands and nature reserves

The wetlands host a wide variety of bog-moss species, heathers, and sedges, while the mildness and humidity of the southwest (in places like Cork and Kerry) encourage a rich array of plants. There are many tropical gardens that make the most of this temperate weather. Once there were extensive oak forests across the country but by the 1600s most of them had been cleared. However, recent re-afforestation has encouraged the return of various types of spruce, pine, larch, and fir trees. In the Burren (a landscape region in northwest County Clare), Arctic and Alpine plants survive from the colder times of glacial cover.

Irish bogs are home to swooping dragonflies and delicate damselflies and Ireland's butterflies include red admirals, peacocks, tortoiseshells, holly blues, brimstones, painted ladies, and the rare endangered marsh fritillary.

There are many nature reserves (at least 75) and six national parks where flora and fauna are protected. Ireland offers countless places to explore both landscape and wildlife and in recent years the State forests (comprising 11 large forest parks and over 400 smaller ones) have opened to the public. Other good places to explore include the 560 miles (900km) or so of the Ulster Way, a meandering circular route that loops its way through many rural areas in Northern Ireland, with wonderful views of coastline, rivers, loughs, farms, and docklands.

Right: Waterlilies flourish on wetlands that gleam high in the wild Connemara moors. The wind ripples the grasses in a bog-dappled peat landscape while purple-flowering heather blooms on the hills.

Opposite above: Irish wetlands are vitally important areas for a wide range of plants and animals. They provide key habitats for the conservation of invertebrates, such as crayfish, and many insects depend on marshy pools and streams for their larval stages.

Opposite below: The caterpillar of the painted lady butterfly (also known as the cosmopolitan) builds a silky webbed nest. It feeds on thistles, mallows, and other plants in the Burren.

Above: On the southern shores of Belfast Lough, a stream meanders through woodland in Crawfordsburn Country Park. The park includes a Countryside Center Exhibition, rugged coastline, two superb beaches, a waterfall tumbling into the deep wooded glen, a pond, meadows glowing with wildflowers and, at Grey Point Fort, a 20th-century coastal battery and gun emplacement.

Left: Rugged mountains sweep down to a lake, their lower slopes covered in trees. The 26,000-acre (10,236-hectare) Killarney National Park (designated a UNESCO Biosphere Reserve in 1981) is a fine mix of lakes, waterfalls, and woodland (some with native oaks and yew) where red deer roam wild and many species of bird are seen.

Coast and river

On the beaches people are often seen digging for cockles and clams or wading into the shallow water to spear turbot. Swimming away from the ocean and upstream into Ireland's rushing freshwater rivers are sea trout and Atlantic salmon that make long migrations to reach the shallow waters where they can safely lay their eggs. These fish may be returning from the saltwater seas round places like Greenland to the same freshwater tributary in which they were born, perhaps three or four years earlier. Throughout their lives, while they have been concentrating on consuming everything from mayflies and crustaceans to Arctic squid and herrings, their numbers will have been decimated by other predatory fish and marine mammals — and birds such as herons, cormorants, and gulls. Now the determined upstream passage of the silvery survivors tempts keen anglers, who may also catch pike, perch, bream, rudd, and sometimes mullet. The teeming river estuaries entice both sporting and professional fisherfolk while, farther inland, other freshwater fish to tempt anglers include char, eel, and brown trout.

Bird life

About 380 species of wild birds fly in the skies or haunt the waterways, 135 of which breed in Ireland. Common mallard and teal nest here and are faithful residents at wetlands all year round, while many birds overwinter in woodland, field, marsh, and lake, some relishing the provender that they can find in harvested oat fields. Migrating visitors include pink-footed and greylag geese from Iceland and the Arctic regions while in fall other 'foreign' birds flock in from Iceland, Canada and Scandinavia, including some three-quarters of the globe's population of Greenland white-fronted geese. Inland waterways support colonies of swans, geese, waders, ducks, terns, and gulls … and wherever you go there is likely to be a 'twitcher' clutching binoculars and camera, always anxious to observe some of the rarer species, like merlins, peregrine falcons, corncrakes, and choughs.

Opposite: White's Castle is found at Athy on the River Barrow.

Below: A female mallard; these ducks inhabit most Irish wetlands.

Creatures banished, isolated, and extinct

There are no snakes here — these were reputedly banished from Ireland long ago by Saint Patrick. The common lizard is Ireland's sole native reptile and, with regard to amphibians, there is only one species of frog — the widespread common frog. Ireland's single toad species is the natterjack toad, found only in Kerry and at Raven Point in County Wexford. Creatures that developed natively in glorious isolation include the Irish stoat and the Irish hare while one of Ireland's past glories, now well and truly extinct, was the Irish elk *(Megaloceros giganteus)*. It was hunted here in prehistoric times. This vast deer — as big as a horse — stood nearly 7ft (over 2m) at the shoulder and proudly challenged intruders with antlers that spanned over 11ft (3m) across. It became extinct in Ireland about 11,000 years ago but specimens of their impressive skulls and great antlers still adorn many a wall in Irish castles and hunting lodges.

Common Irish mammals

Sadly, wolves and golden eagles no longer haunt the landscape but some 30 or so mammal species do still enjoy the temperate seas and landscapes of Ireland. The American mink has successfully introduced itself into the Irish environment and is now firmly established. Specimens originally escaped from mink farms; unfortunately they now pose a threat to local wildlife — particularly birds, such as coots, moorhens, and the rare red-throated divers. Other mammals include red foxes, badgers, otters, hares, rabbits, deer, and red squirrels.

Above: The shy and elusive river otter lives and hunts in many Irish lakes and rivers.

Opposite above: Long ago, red squirrels were common in Ireland but they became extinct by about 1700. They were reintroduced some 200 years ago and their numbers soon recovered.

Opposite right: Common frogs are seen (or heard!) in every Irish county.

Opposite left: On sunny days, the common lizard — Ireland's only reptile — suns itself on warm stone walls, rocks, or logs.

Left: This red fox shows his canine teeth as he catches his breath in a field of oats.

Hills and mountains

Laced with silvery streams and small wriggling roads, the Sperrins are one of Ireland's largest upland areas and comprise a rugged spike of mountains, bogland, and inland waters interspersed with some more gently contoured peaty hills. This stretch of mountain landscape arcs across some 20 miles (32km) southeast of Derry in Northern Ireland. The highest peaks (Sawel, Mullaclogher, and Mullaghaneany) all rise above 2000ft (600m) with crystalline limestone caps and valleys scoured out by long-vanished glaciers. Brilliant yellow gorse flowers lend an unexpectedly bright golden splash almost all year, scenting the air with their sweet smell which is reminiscent of coconuts. Sometimes farmers crush the green spikes to make a mash reputed to give their horses shinier coats — and it is relished by hungry pigs too.

Great oaks and lofty elms dot the more fertile valleys. In Northern Ireland, located between Cookstown and Stewartstown, is tree-ringed Tullaghoge hill. Its summit provides a fine view of the old kingdom of Tyrone where, from the 11th century onward, chiefs of the O'Neill clan were crowned … *amid the clang of bucklers and a hundred harps* … as the chosen heir sat poised on a stone throne. New sandals were placed upon his feet as the gathered chiefs chanted his name. Tullaghoge fort is an enclosure that may have emerged from a pagan sanctuary and it is encircled by two banks and ditches with a causeway entrance. This was a royal stronghold rather than a fortified farmstead.

Sacred mountain

Croagh Patrick in County Mayo is the sacred mountain where Saint Patrick is believed to have fasted for 40 days and nights and the place from where he banished snakes. (The symbol of the Druid faith was a snake so, in fact, this action may be a metaphor for the overthrow of the old pagan beliefs.) Each year on Reek Sunday, the last Sunday of July, thousands of people — many of them barefoot — trek up a loose scree pathway to the 2510ft (765m) peak.

Right: Sheep graze near the Sperrin Mountains (their name derived from Na Speiríní meaning 'Spurs of Rock'). Rivers teem with life and the once-glaciated landscape is now a veritable patchwork quilt of field, forest, marsh, and lake below often snowcapped peaks.

Following pages: The conical peak of Croagh Patrick in County Mayo soars majestically above the surrounding countryside. This is an ancient place of worship and the remains of a Celtic hill fort encircling the summit have been discovered here.

Killarney in County Kerry boasts Ireland's highest peak, Carrantuohill, rising to 3414ft (1040m). It is part of the rugged 12-mile (19km) long Macgillicuddy's Reeks (or the Black Stacks). This glacially carved sandstone ridge stretches along the Iveragh peninsula on Ireland's southwestern tip, where the foothills are lush with rich woodlands. Here too are the peaks of Beenkeragh at 3314ft (1010m), Caher at 3284ft (1001m), and more than 100 other summits rising above 2000ft (610m).

The cone-shaped peak of Errigal in Donegal's Derryveagh Mountains in northwest Ireland soars up to some 2467ft (752m) and is another of Ireland's highest summits. It stands at the southwestern end of a quartzite high-peaked ridge where the ruined village church of Dunlewy was built in local sugary white marble. Muckish Mountain in the Derryveagh range is a high plateau that offers a superb vantage point from which to survey Donegal's patchwork quilt of fields, lakes, and hills. Set above the lush landscape of County Galway, the Twelve Bens rise rugged with rocky quartzite outcrops and are dotted with villages, lonely homesteads, and abandoned ruins.

The Derryveagh range includes Slieve Snaght (snowy mountain) as its highest peak. This area was scoured wide and deep long millennia ago by a glacier, one among many that formed the pattern of valleys and rocks in Donegal and Mayo (and the Scottish Highlands too). Here the Poisoned Glen fosters many unusual plants beside a little stream that meanders over the peaty moorland. Its present name came about because an English cartographer misspelled the Irish word for heaven *(neamh)* as *neimhe* (meaning poison) so the Heavenly Glen gained a rather less alluring title — but it remains a most beautiful place.

Above: *Steep Mount Errigal (2467ft/752m high) and flat-topped Muckish (meaning 'pig's back') rise high in County Donegal's Derryveagh Mountains. Both are part of a chain known locally as the Seven Sisters.*

Left: *Killarney National Park was Ireland's first, established in 1932. The nation's only native herd of red deer roam wild in natural forest here.*

Opposite: *Macgillycuddy's Reeks (County Kerry) are called Na Cruacha Dubha in Irish, meaning 'The Black Stacks.' This chain includes Ireland's highest mountain, Carrantuohill, which rises to 3414ft (1040m).*

The Mountains of Mourne

The Kingdom of Mourne provides a backdrop of lovely mountains in the southern part of County Down in Northern Ireland — a lonely area of granite mountains slashed by quarry workings. These wild peaks rise majestically behind beaches, deep forests, and lush green fields — their beauty forever immortalized by Irish songwriter Percy French in his song *The Mountains of Mourne*. Here, deriving their name from *sliabh* (meaning mountain) are Slieve Donard, Slieve Lamagan, and Slieve Muck — as well as the Mourne Wall, a dry-stone wall built between 1904 and 1922 to enclose the water catchment area and to provide work during a period of high unemployment; it wriggles across 15 summits and encloses the Silent Valley Reservoir (see page 102). Mountainous terrain includes the towering Castle and Diamond Rocks.

Mysterious Ben Bulben, looming flat-topped from the Sligo plain, is associated with Saint Columba, the poet W.B. Yeats, and with legends about how the mythical hunter Finn McCool failed to heal one of his warriors, Diarmuid, when the brave fighter was fatally gored by a gigantic wild enchanted boar that they had been hunting on the heath here.

Left: A crumbling cottage in the Mourne Mountains where some peaks have evocative names — Buzzard's Roost, Brandy Pad, Devil's Coach Road, Percy Bysshe, Pigeon Rock, and Pollaphuca (meaning 'hole of the fairies').

Background: The 1014ft (327m) limestone Knocknarea Mountain rises above Strandhill in County Sligo.

Opposite below: The Mourne Mountains are enchantingly beautiful. Heathers, thyme, harebells, and orchids bloom here as falcons and buzzards soar above.

Below: Ben Bulben (County Sligo) inspired Nobel Literature prizewinner and celebrated poet, W.B. Yeats. In 1948 his remains were laid to rest in Drumcliff churchyard in the shadow of the great mountain.

The Burren

This strange landscape of contorted rocks and hillocks in County Clare is a limestone plateau measuring about 116sq miles (300km²) or so, formed some 350 million years ago. Its limestone pavements are riven by cracks called 'grikes' that form isolated 'clint' rocks. Few trees survive but many amazing Mediterranean, Arctic, and Alpine wildflowers (such as gentians) do flourish well, despite the stern and seemingly inhospitable habitat. One of Oliver Cromwell's generals, Edmund Ludlow, wrote in the 1640s that it was … *a savage land, yielding neither water enough to drown a man, nor a tree to hang him, nor soil enough to bury him …*

This is an excellent area for potholing, rock-climbing and visiting ancient burial sites (see also page 50). Over 90 megalithic tombs are scattered throughout the Burren, as well as many dolmens and ring forts — including the triple ring fort of Cahercommaun, set on the edge of an inland cliff. The (at least) 5000-year-old Poulnabrone dolmen (or 'The Hole of the Sorrows') has high portal stones supporting a slice of capstone. The site has yielded many burial finds including the uncremated remains of a newborn baby, six youngsters, and about 20 adults … plus flint arrowheads and scrapers, a polished stone ax, and pottery shards.

The Doorty Cross is a splendid Celtic high cross found at Kilfenora in County Clare by a cathedral built between 1189 and 1200. Once there were seven crosses here and it was known as the city of the crosses. The 13ft (4m) high cross that remains dates back to the 12th century; its finely detailed carvings depict three people, including the original bishop here, Saint Fachtnan.

Opposite: The Burren — its name derives from the Irish bhoireann *meaning a stony place. This ancient plateau is the largest area of karstic limestone in western Europe. Many rare plants flourish here.*

Below: The gray limestone Burren plateau rises beyond woodland and a winding road in County Clare.

Moors, bogs, and marshes

The moors of western Ulster were once home to many impoverished Irish people, some driven there by English landlords. Many starved to death. A few left the country to sail away to a better life elsewhere or to enlist in foreign armies.

Moors and upland heaths are the most likely places to spot the increasingly rare Irish red grouse *(Lagopus lagopus hibernicus)*. The males are pale reddish brown and the females have yellower plumage, both having finely barred markings that help to camouflage them in grasses and sedge. Surrounded by coniferous forest, the upland moor of Slieveannora is one place where heather forms a major part of the grouse diet and also offers vital hidey-holes in which to secrete nests. The birds prefer heather moors away from trees but may also be found in bogs — low-lying, blanket, or raised — or as an occasional farm visitor when the weather is severe. The grouse population is declining seriously, and careful management and conservation of habitats like this is an important way of stabilizing their numbers.

Ireland is renowned for its boglands: many of them are raised bogs — rich in flora, fauna, and archeological remains — extending across Kildare, Offaly, and Laois. Raised bogs rise on dead layers of sphagnum moss and are found in low-lying areas. Their central portion is raised like a dome, which accounts for their name. Blanket bogs consist of the remains of grasses and sedges and usually form in upland areas. For years these boglands have proved a marvelous source of peat that is found only in areas where high rainfall and low temperatures combine in waterlogged sites. Used as a fuel for many centuries before it gained its more recent popularity as a garden soil enhancer, now it is gradually being appreciated that, worldwide, peat is a diminishing and irreplaceable commodity. In Ireland it was laid down after the Ice Age in about 7000 BC. The cutting of peat turfs for fuel has long been an industry here.

Stone Age people arrived in Ireland some 6000 years ago and, ever since, local farmers have grazed their herds on the peatlands while the wild animals, birds, and wild berries provided a source of food for the first dwellers here. Peat was used as a fuel from at least the 7th century and by the 18th century its fibers also served as a source of material for making wrapping paper and postcards!

Right: Mounds of peat have been cut from this bog in County Galway. Relative to its size, Ireland has a greater proportion of bog than any country in Europe except Finland — 4633sq miles (1,200,000 hectares) or one-sixth of the island.

Above: Deep crimson succulent cranberries flourish in the Irish boglands.

Left: Sparkling water-like drops on the carnivorous sundew plant attract insects to their fate on its sticky, sensitive tentacles.

Wildlife habitat

Cranberry and bog rosemary flourish on the raised boglands while on the blanket bogs, tawny grasses and cottongrass toss and shimmer above mosses, lichens, and grassy hummocks beside natural drains, swallow holes, and lakes that are dotted with islands. Bright flowers decorate the landscape. Typically found growing here are ling heather, bog asphodel, purple moor grass, black bog rush, bog-cotton, and deer sedge, while insectivorous sundews and butterworts survive by trapping small flying creatures with their sticky leaves. Bladderworts in gleaming pools suck in microscopic animal life through their trapdoors that are activated when a prey animal brushes against trigger-hairs.

Both types of bog provide excellent habitats for many small mammals, birds, frogs, slugs, and countless insects. Birds may include little and great crested grebes, lapwings and snipe, Greenland white-fronted geese, merlins, and golden plovers.

Dramatic Céide Fields in County Mayo combines bogland with spectacular soaring cliffs where 300-million-year-old rocks rise almost 400ft (122m) high. This is a suitably impressive setting for the most extensive Stone Age monument in the world (see page 56).

Background: A track leads through a peat bog in County Sligo. Today many areas of raised bog are preserved as Sites of Special Scientific Interest.

Rivers of Ireland

The Shannon is the longest river in Ireland (and Great Britain too), flowing along a 240-mile (386km) course as it divides the western and midland regions of the Emerald Isle. Legends tell how salmon once swallowed scarlet berries that fell from an overhanging rowan tree into a well and in this manner gained both red spots and great wisdom. According to legend, the River Shannon is named for a woman called Sionan who caught and ate a salmon from this well when women were forbidden from doing so, causing a great flood to burst from the well and carry her in its flow westward to the sea. Many salmon still congregate in the river and are said to whisper Sionan's name. The river reaches the Atlantic Ocean beyond the city of Limerick. On its long journey it is overlooked by historic towns, castles, and monasteries on riverbanks where marshy grasslands or bogs bustle with wildlife and birds.

It is the lovely Liffey that courses through Dublin. It has many busy quays and is criss-crossed by numerous bridges. It rises in the mountains of County Wicklow some 20 miles (32km) southwest of Dublin and flows on for 75 miles (125km) through Counties Kildare and Dublin to reach the Irish Sea in Dublin Bay. It has been the main artery of the city since the Vikings steered their longships into its estuary almost 1200 years ago and has been a major shipping lane ever since. James Joyce identified the river with Anna Livia Plurabelle, the main female presence in his novel *Finnegan's Wake*.

Another major river is the Barrow. Its riverbanks are lined with reeds and villages as it courses for 119 miles (192km) from source to sea, through 23 Victorian locks and major river ports at Athy (where it joins the Grand Canal), Carlow, Graiguenamanagh, and New Ross. Once barges carried malting barley along it to Dublin to make the famous Guinness stout — which was then transported back downstream — or took beet to Ireland's first sugar factory at Carlow.

Ancient waterway

Thousands of years ago, the 70-mile (112km) long River Boyne was used to transport the rocks for megalithic tombs. It now flows past many historic places including the famous 1690 Battle of the Boyne site (near Drogheda), the ancient city of Trim with its castle, the Hill of Tara (once the capital of the High King of Ireland) and the well-preserved passage tombs at Newgrange (see page 22).

Here too stands Mellifont Abbey, Ireland's earliest Cistercian abbey founded in 1142 and the medieval city of Drogheda. The many historical attractions here include the Kells Heritage Center (in the town where the Book of Kells

originated), Celtic crosses, King John's Castle at Trim, the lovely abbey at Bective in County Meath, and the towering hill of Slane, where Saint Patrick lit a Paschal flame to defy nearby pagan kings. Successive Viking raids failed to overthrow the monastery that is still standing on this hill.

Above: The River Shannon, Ireland's longest, sweeps past Limerick Castle. The Shannon begins its journey in the Cuilcagh Mountains of County Fermanagh, Northern Ireland, from where it flows through Shannon Cave, and rises at Shannon Pot in County Cavan continuing its course through, or between, 13 of Ireland's counties.

Opposite: The River Barrow is Ireland's second longest river after the River Shannon. It is seen here near Graiguenamanagh, where one of its many locks is situated.

Above: Glowering clouds lend dramatic impact to Trim Castle, perched beside the River Boyne. The famous Battle of the Boyne took place beside this river near Drogheda in 1690.

The Blackwater River is one of Ireland's longest at 104 miles (167km). It rises in County Kerry, forms the boundary between Kerry and County Cork, and then flows east, eventually reaching the sea at Youghal, County Cork, where, at its broadest point, the estuary is almost a mile across. The Blackwater is renowned for its prolific salmon fishing (as well as roach and dace) and is also home to large flocks of wading birds, egret colonies, and otters that feast on the plentiful fish.

Other important rivers include the clean, roach-filled Inny, with its many small rapids and the Lee that rises in the Shehy mountains and flows through Cork. The 87-mile (140km) long Nore, renowned for its salmon and trout, is one of the Three Sisters rivers (with the Barrow and Suir) that rise in County Tipperary and flow into the sea at Waterford. The broad 114-mile (183km) River Suir passes by rich farmland, rustling rushes, and tree-lined banks, attracting anglers keen to fly-fish for wild brown trout. The River Swilly rises near Glendore Mountain in County Donegal and flows for some 26 miles (42km), passing Letterkenny before reaching the Atlantic Ocean at the head of Lough Swilly.

Canals

Canals have played their part here too and, from the 1800s, such waterways connected the River Shannon with Dublin, providing vital transport routes until the railroad — and then road haulage — fulfilled this role. But long before the era of cars, trains, or barges, when horned helmets were the rage, Vikings took advantage of many Irish waterways from about AD 795 to launch fierce raids into Ireland and occupy land.

Warbands roamed and pillaged along these waterways until, in the 10th century, Viking sea-king Thormodr Helgason set up a base on the west coast whence he attacked Ireland all along the River Shannon, pillaging churches, ecclesiastical settlements and taking their accumulated wealth. By as early as AD 822, Viking raids were an annual occurrence around the coast and rivers but eventually infighting diminished the Viking hold; when warriors from Limerick clashed with their Dublin counterparts on Lough Ree in both 937 and 943, the Viking stronghold was diminished.

The true end of Viking rule came in 980 when the Norsemen were heavily defeated at Tara by the armies of Brian Ború but, by then, the Scandinavians had become integrated into the Irish way of life, building settlements, marrying local women, and often converting to Christianity. In this way, although the Viking stranglehold was relaxed, their heritage remained. They left much treasure in their wake too; major archeological finds have revealed gold Norse ingots, bracelets and armbands, including possibly the largest hoard of Viking gold yet discovered (found in 1802) up the River Shannon at Hare Island. There are over 50 small islands on the lake here. They were inhabited by monks before the Viking seizure, and Hare Island was where Saint Ciaran lived before he founded the renowned monastic site of Clonmacnoise in 545.

Above: The River Lee flows eastward through the city of Cork.

Opposite: Sunset glows gold behind a Dublin canal lock. The city's waterways are often busy with barges, waterfowl, and anglers.

Irish Loughs

There are a number of sizable lakes (called loughs here) along Ireland's rivers, with freshwater Lough Neagh being not only Ireland's biggest at 151sq miles (392km^2) but also one of Europe's 40 largest. It lies about 19 miles (30km) to the west of Belfast. Like the Giant's Causeway, in legends Lough Neagh was created as a result of giant jealousy. Legends tell how Finn McCool was fighting with a rival in Scotland, and he threw a huge scoop of earth at him. It fell into the Irish Sea — this made the Isle of Man while the hole left behind filled with water to become Lough Neagh.

The River Shannon boasts three loughs: Allen, Ree, and Derg (the biggest). Other large lakes include beautiful Lough Erne in Fermanagh, actually a pair of lakes linked by tributaries and pools. On its 154 islands many wildflowers and birds thrive, including swans, terns, sandpipers, nightjars, garden warblers, herons, and great crested grebes. Many of the little isles boast Christian or pagan monuments, such as the 12th-century round tower on Devenish Island. The 77sq miles (200km^2) of Lough Corrib lies in western Ireland near where the River Corrib meets the sea.

Across on the eastern side of Ireland, amid the Mourne Mountains — designated an Area of Outstanding Natural Beauty — lies the stunning Silent Valley reservoir, formed by the Crom Dam that stems the flow of the River Kilkeel to provide Belfast with water.

Above: An old abbey on Devenish Island in Lower Lough Erne, one of Northern Ireland's finest monastic sites. It also boasts a wonderful 12th-century round tower and the remains of the Oratory of St Molaise who established the 6th-century monastery.

Opposite: A boat is moored on a peaceful Killarney lake; the three famous lakes here are Lough Leane (the Lower Lake and largest, near Killarney town), Muckross (or Middle) Lake, and Upper Lake.

Below: A sunset gilds the ripples on Lower Lough Erne. This is one of the UK's largest freshwater lakes and is home to snipe, curlews, lapwings, grebes, redshanks, whooper swans, and terns.

Left: *This traditional whitewashed waterside cottage is set upon springy turf beside a peaceful lake in rugged Connemara with majestic mountains close by. It is an idyllic spot for a restful holiday, for keen anglers to test their skills, or for artists and photographers to try to capture the glorious landscape with its ever-changing moods and patterns of light.*

Top: *Lough Derg on the River Shannon is the second largest lake in the Republic of Ireland and is renowned for its superb game and coarse fishing. In the 19th century it formed an important artery from the port at Limerick and linked to the canals in the midlands of Ireland which enabled navigation right through to Dublin.*

Above: *A rowing boat is moored in the shallows of Lough Corrib — the largest lough in the Republic of Ireland.*

Wetland wildlife

Ireland's climate is dominated by the warm Gulf Stream, and the mild wet winters provide ideal wintering conditions for wildfowl. Huge flocks arrive here to join resident ducks and waders on loughs and estuaries. Over half the world's population of Greenland white-fronted geese fly into the Wexford Wildfowl Reserve which is situated on a large area of reclaimed wetland. It is also visited by brent and greylag geese, while barnacle geese are a common sight on the west coast.

Atlantic salmon and sea trout swim upriver from the ocean to spawn, sometimes leaping up waterfalls and surging rivers to lay their eggs in the loughs. Here too are found pike, perch, bream, and rudd, while the river estuaries are home to mullet and plaice. Rich wetlands support pochard (diving ducks), moorhens, woodcock, and snipe, while common mallard and teal nest on inland waterways. Fall sees flocks of visiting geese arriving on the river marshes. All year round, peregrine falcons hunt among mountain crags and scoured quarries.

Wet conditions encourage a profusion of plants, such as water lobelia that holds its pale lilac flowers on slim scarlet stalks above the shallows of stony lakes; and fleabane (once used to repel fleas) that grows in meadows and marshes where it flaunts its bright yellow flowers. A thriving insect life is found here too and places like the Buncrana wildlife sanctuary in Donegal offers visitors the chance to see hundreds of insects and butterflies as well as 130 bird and 20 mammal species and a profusion of plants and trees.

Inch Level (6 miles/10km south of Buncrana) is one of the most important wetlands in the northwest and has been granted international ecological status. It is a permanent home for mute swans and also plays temporary host to whooper and Bewick swans.

Ireland's native otter *(Lutra lutra)* is a member of the weasel family, a sleek brown creature with an inquisitive face, gorgeous whiskers, and sensitive hairs framing its snout which help it to locate its prey. It flourishes in all types of wetland environments including rivers, streams, lakes, marshes, and ditches, as well as in coastal areas. Its aquatic lifestyle is helped by its webbed feet, the ability to close both ears and nose when under water, and dense short fur that traps an extra layer of insulating air close to its body. Otters communicate with high-pitched whistles, twitterings, and cat-like mews. Their home (called a holt) is usually a snug hole under tree roots in a bank or under a bridge.

Opposite left: The name foxglove is a corruption of 'folks' gloves' — an allusion to the wee folk who were said to use the purple flowers as gloves. The Latin name, Digitalis, describes the finger-like blooms.

Opposite right: A shallow stream courses its slow passage through marshy terrain and water-loving grasses and reeds in Annascaul, on the Dingle peninsula.

Left: A common blue butterfly settles on yellow fleabane, concealing its violet-blue coloration as it closes its wings. On sunny days small groups of these butterflies may gather together to feed.

Below: A moorhen safeguards its nest, its distinctive red bill a bright flash against glossy black feathers. This is actually a ground-dwelling bird but is usually found near water and is a good swimmer.

Field and farm

The ancient Gaelic peoples led a pastoral existence usually involving small-scale tilling, subsistence farming, and the nurture of a vital herd of cattle to provide milk, butter, and a rough cheese called milsen. The herds were moved out to the hills or summer pastures on May Day and brought back in again as winter began. A bull and breeding cows would be fed and overwintered; calves were slaughtered and eaten.

Pork was a much-prized meat, eaten fresh at feasts or salted to preserve for later consumption. The old laws dictated that at night pigs must be secured by collars in their sties. They were fattened on mast (nuts, acorns, etc.) in the woodlands and forests and slaughtered in the fall; just the sows and one sire were overwintered. November saw the ceremonial slaughtering of a cock and the sprinkling of its blood on the threshold, house corners, and hearth before it was boiled and eaten, with some of the flesh given to the first beggar that passes, in honor of Saint Martin, patron saint of the poor.

Herb gardens provided leeks, onions, and garlic while cabbage, watercress, seaweed, and nettle porridge were also relished. Wheat and rye were cultivated — with beer being brewed from barley and the best bread made from wheat. Irish mills relied on waterpower to turn the millstones that ground the wheat into flour for baking.

Agriculture through history

It was the Vikings who introduced the first tilled oblong fields (called stangs), worked by plow horses. Field rotation arrived with the Normans; each manor or parish tilled one large field, used the second for pasture, and left the third fallow. There were also meadows, orchards, and coneywarrens for rabbits. Cistercian monasteries pioneered more commercial farming, with the monks viewing this labor as an equivalent form of prayer. They maintained large granges, vast herds of sheep as well as eel and salmon fisheries. In mid- and western Ulster, the old Gaelic system of agriculture continued until the early 17th century.

Between 1554 and 1660, English and Scots planters took charge in certain areas. Ulster forests were cleared so the land could be tilled; cherry and cider-apple trees were planted — and the potato arrived. In 1654, the Cromwellian plantation transferred the ownership of most of the land owned by Catholics to the planters (colonists from England). Irish laborers now worked for these new masters. After 1760 there was more intensive farming as fences surrounded fields, butter markets sprang up, and cattle export expanded now that the beasts could be overwintered while fed on turnips. Cattle, meat, wheat, linen, and butter were transported via rivers or canals to both domestic and export markets.

In the 18th century, flax (the raw material for linen) was an important crop, used at home for clothes, household linen, and sail making, as well as being exported.

Right: This view from the Sugar Loaf in County Wicklow shows rolling hills and a patchwork of brown, green, russet, and gold fields — their edges laced with hedges and trees. Times are changing and today the easier city lifestyle lures people away from the land, and so farming is in decline.

Left: Cattle have long been an important part of Irish farming and are a common sight in the lush pastures and stone-walled fields. Iron-Age Celts reared cattle to provide milk, butter, cheese, and meat, and their wealth was measured by the number of cows they owned.

Following pages: As summer peaks, bright poppies make a scarlet blaze among the crops in many Irish fields.

Towns, villages, and old manorial estates held frequent fairs to which cattle, sheep, and pigs were driven for sale. Poor tenants and laborers lived in mud-walled thatched cabins, raising cattle and crops, burdened by heavy rents and annual Church tithes — and dependent on the potato for food. It was hard to eke out a living on land that was often poor and infertile and there were many evictions and feuds as a result. Meanwhile cheap imported American grain rendered wheat-growing unprofitable, oats were used to feed the horses and (as porridge or small cakes) served for human consumption too, but the potato was still the staple food. When the potato crop failed through blight, this had a catastrophic impact and ultimately the Great Famine led to dire starvation in the 1840s.

Agricultural machinery, such as hay-cutting machines, arrived during the 1870s, but this trend was initially strongly opposed by the laborers. From 1885 onward, a series of Acts of Parliament enabled farmers to buy land with money advanced by the British government and repaid in yearly instalments. The Irish Land Act of 1881 meant that farm laborers were properly housed at last — often in better homes than the farmers. In due course, co-operative creameries encouraged dairy farming while their shops sold seeds, farm implements, groceries and clothes at a fair price.

In the 1930s, when horse-pulled reaper-and-binder machines for corn appeared, Eamon De Valera's government refused to pay the British government land annuities until a 1938 treaty settled matters. During World War Two, cattle, sheep, pigs, butter, and tinned milk were exported to war-struck England. In due course new machinery like combine harvesters reduced the need for farm labor so many young people moved away from the land into towns or emigrated to England. Old-style fairs were replaced by cattle marts — except for a few annual horsefairs that were still held each year. Finally, in 1973, Ireland joined the EEC. Now farmers were supported with grants while smaller creameries and farms were consolidated. A new and more prosperous rural way of life was established.

Right: The last rays of the day's sunlight struggle to cling onto this typical Irish farming landscape in County Wicklow.

Below: Here in County Sligo farmers plowed in the traditional way, using horse power. Shires, Suffolks, and Clydesdales were once numerous in Ireland but there were also indigenous workhorses that differed from the traditional British breeds; these were the Irish Drafts which were thoroughbreds crossed with farm horses.

Countryside creatures

Mammals in the Irish countryside include red foxes that grow thicker winter russet fur, which is one reason why they have been hunted. However, farmers have always seen the fox as a cunning poultry-killing pest and so it has been consistently chased, shot, poisoned, snared, and trapped as well as being hunted for sport. Nonetheless, the fox is an amazing and adaptable survivor that lives in towns too. Dublin, for instance, has a healthy population of urban foxes right across the city and suburbs.

Badgers are distributed throughout Ireland, usually living in groups of up to 15 in a system of underground tunnels and chambers called a sett. It is snugly lined with moss and grass and is often used by a succession of generations, as are their foraging routes along which they seek a plentiful supply of earthworms, plus beetles, voles, mice, frogs, snails, acorns, fruits, and roots.

Irish fields are home to hares and rabbits too — the Irish hare *(Lepus timidus hibernicus)*, the brown hare *(Lepus europaeus* or *Lepus capensis)* and the rabbit *(Oryctolagus cuniculus)* are all found here. Brown (or 'thrush') hares were introduced here by 19th-century landowners for hunting but did not adapt well, so remain scarce. The native Irish hare, however, is a sturdy survivor: stocky, with black-tipped ears and long back legs, it is found throughout Ireland. It becomes paler in winter with whitish underparts and legs. Hares box upright prior to mating and then conceal their two or three litters a year in vegetation, preferring 'unimproved' land not subject to modern farming practices. They live out in the open but dig shallow 'forms' in which to rest with their backs against the wind. Rabbits were introduced to Ireland by the Normans in the 1100s. They live in enclosed warrens in dry ground. They have several litters each year from the age of around three months and are most active from dawn to dusk. Vixens may use old rabbit warrens to rear their cubs safely.

Hares and rabbits also have a place in Irish mythology. Early pagan gods who were worshipped in Ireland included the moon goddess Eostre. Her festival was celebrated in the spring and was inspired by the shape of a hare or rabbit carrying an egg that could sometimes be detected in the moon's patterned surface. The hare was believed to be the earthly form of Eostre, ever gazing up at her lunar home. In Christian times, this practice mutated into the tradition of Easter eggs, rabbits, and hares.

Opposite: Badgers roam through the wild woods, often close to pastureland, and live in setts with separate nesting chambers for their spring litters of two or three cubs. They are nocturnal, coming out at night to play and feed. Badgers growl or bark warnings and may 'purr' with pleasure.

Left: Brown hares leap across open grassland but prefer to rest by day in woodland and hedgerows. Their spring courtship involves boxing when unreceptive females fend off males — hence the term 'mad as a March hare.' Females may have three litters a year; the leverets will be weaned at about a month.

Below: A wary fox checks its surroundings; this adaptable animal can live in many climates, terrains, and habitats — including urban areas — and is an opportunistic feeder, upturning litter bins or hunting live prey.

Trees and woodlands

In prehistoric times there were primeval forests all over Ireland. Woodlands here reached their maximum cover some 7000 years ago with the most common trees being oak, elm, ash, Scots pine, and alder. Then, some 5000-6000 years ago, farmers began to clear the land. By Celtic times much of the forest had gone. Then trees and woodland plants were protected by the Brehon Law (part of the code of early Irish law), especially the seven so-called 'nobles of the wood' — oak, hazel, holly, yew, ash, Scots pine, and crab-apple. Damage to one of these trees would result in a fine of a three-year-old heifer and two milch cows. Nonetheless, tree clearance accelerated from the 1500s when the ruling English took timber for building, industry, and fuel. By the 1900s, only about 0.5 percent (86,500 acres/35,000 hectares) of the land was under trees. Surviving woodlands included Glenconkeyne (near Lough Neagh). However, the new settlers promptly chopped down the oak trees here and floated the logs downriver for the building of Coleraine and Limavady.

Today planting has increased woodland cover to over 1.5 million acres (600,000 hectares) although that total includes 84 percent non-native conifer species. The timber is used for fuel, tool-making, or building — and the woodlands contain up to 5000 species of plants and animals. Great gnarled oak trees, ash, alder, and the occasional elm flourish — as does other diverse flora, such as bamboos, ferns, huge rhododendrons, foxgloves, fuchsias, vivid golden gorse, and delicate orchids and gentians. Several woodlands (such as Rostrevor Forest in Mourne and Gosford Forest Park in Armagh) are nature reserves. Killarney National Park in southwest Ireland was Ireland's first (and is now its largest) national park, covering over 25,000 acres (10,000 hectares) of mountain, park, woodland, waterway, and moorland. Here are mountainous red sandstone uplands, blanket bogs, yew woodlands, oakwoods, and many elegant red deer roaming wild.

In single-species woodlands, Sitka spruce and lodgepole pine are often grown, creating an evergreen canopy so that little light reaches the ground. Once the plantations are thinned, however, clearing encourages a new spurt of heather and foxgloves to grow, while animals such as deer crop below treetops that serve as lookout posts for many birds. The beady-eyed pine marten scurries about in the undergrowth and is an agile tree climber whose diet includes other small mammals as well as birds and insects.

Oak and hazel have always been highly prized in Ireland. There are hazel scrubs in the Burren (County Clare) where the shallow soil and harsh prevailing winds prevent trees growing above 10 to 13ft (3 to 4m) high. In the rich carpet of moss below, emerald ferns uncurl and wild flowers bloom.

Opposite: A woodland stream courses through Sheffrey Woods in County Mayo where, in the damp atmosphere, moss coats boulders and bark in thick green cushions.

Below: A stunted hawthorn tree in Connemara National Park where blanket bog and heathland are the most common vegetation.

Creatures of the forest

Forest fauna includes the red squirrel population (albeit now in decline), the largest and most regal deer, the red deer *(Cervus elaphus)* that became extinct in Ireland but has now been re-introduced, fallow deer *(Dama dama)* brought to the British Isles by the Romans and introduced into Irish forests in the 13th century, and — the most recent addition — sika deer *(Cervus nippon)*, brought here from Japan in the late 19th century. These are the smallest Irish deer: males measure about 33in (85cm) to the shoulder. Fallow deer grow to around 35in (90cm) and reds reach 47in (120cm).

Smaller woodland inhabitants include the wood mouse or long-tailed field mouse *(Apodemus sylvaticus)*. These shy, secretive creatures are rarely seen — with good reason as they rank high on the menu of many predators (including foxes, stoats, owls, kestrels, and domestic cats). Their large ears and eyes (they have excellent night vision) and an acute sense of smell quickly warn them of intruders. Their own diet includes seeds such as sycamore 'helicopters,' acorns, buds, fruits, berries, fungi, and juicy invertebrates like worms, snails and centipedes. Prolific hoarders, these small rodents store the summer surfeit to supplement shortages in winter when, although they do not hibernate, they live communally in moss, leaf, and grass nests to conserve warmth during cold weather. They make complex networks of underground tunnels with multiple chambers and food stores.

Opposite: Ireland's woods and forests provide a variety of habitats for numerous species of animals and birds.

Left: Through the centuries, many parkland fallow deer escaped to nearby forests where they thrived. Today, new wild populations still spring up from escaped stock.

Below: The barn owl was once a common farmland bird but its numbers are in sharp decline, with a devastating drop in populations over recent years.

From castle to cottage

Ireland's rural landscape is spiked with many fortified towers and castles. The earliest castles were earthwork or timber constructions, and these were followed by great stone structures raised in the 12th century by Anglo-Norman invaders, and defensive fortifications built by Gaelic chieftains. Castle building continued until the late 1600s. Massive castles were succeeded by one- or two-story stronghouses called hall-houses, built as protective barracks for garrisons. Then came the classic Irish tower houses, protected by battlements, but actually serving as family homes for local chieftains and their retinue. They served this purpose until the advent of gunpowder and artillery rendered them more vulnerable to attack. By the late 17th and early 18th century, wealthy landlords were moving out of the old castles into new-built, revivalist, castle-style homes.

Famous Blarney Castle, near Cork, was built nearly six centuries ago by a great chieftain — Cormac MacCarthy, King of Munster. Today it is celebrated for its famous stone — said to provide the gift of gab or 'the privilege of telling lies for seven years.' To attain this verbosity one must kiss the legendary Stone of Eloquence at the top of the tower: this involves bending over backward and hanging onto two handrails while leaning out from the battlements.

Bunratty Castle is Ireland's most complete medieval fortress, built in 1425 and now beautifully restored with medieval furnishings and tapestries. The castle stands amid delightful grounds and has a wonderful walled Victorian-style garden. Thirteenth-century King John's Castle is set on King's Island in the heart of Limerick, overlooking the River Shannon and the city. Its 800-year-old heritage is revealed in the strong fortifications, excavated pre-Norman houses, siege mines, and battlement walks. King John had his own coins struck in the castle mint here.

Opposite: In the 16th century, Queen Elizabeth I sent the Earl of Leicester to seize Blarney Castle. Forever delayed by banquets or other diversions, his long excusatory missives to his irritated queen prompted her to remark that his reports were all 'Blarney.'

Below: Built in 1425, Bunratty Castle, in County Clare, is an impressive tower house with spiral stairs and dungeons.

Background: *King John's Castle overlooks the majestic River Shannon, just north of Limerick's city center. It is a sturdy, five-sided castle with corner towers and a double-towered gatehouse. Built during the reign of King John of England, it served as a royal fortress as well as a regional administration and military center.*

Left: *An engraving of English King John who reigned in England from 1199 to 1216 but was in charge of Irish affairs from 1189 to 1210. While his crusading brother was called Richard the Lionheart, John gained the less flattering nicknames of John Lackland or Softsword — due to his military failings and defeats by the French and his own barons.*

JOHN.

Carrickfergus Castle (see also page 67) is a wonderfully preserved medieval structure, built by John de Courcy in 1177 and was an important English garrison in Ulster. King John laid siege to it in 1210 and it was here that King William III landed in Ireland in 1690.

Dunluce Castle in County Antrim was first built in the 1200s (where once an early Irish ring fort stood) by Richard de Burgh, Earl of Ulster. Surrounded by dizzying drops, the romantic ruins are set on a high basalt stack with a sea cave, called the Mermaid's Cave, below. Often under siege, its precipitous site served the stronghold well, but, in 1584, a Scottish chieftain called Sorley Boy MacDonnell captured it. Then four years later, enriched by Spanish Armada booty seized when the treasure ship *Girona* was wrecked, he modernized the castle. Stories tell how, in 1639, the kitchen fell into the sea — along with the cooks and servants.

Beyond all these castle walls lies the diverse rural scene, pinpricked with farms and cottages (some with thatched roofs), dotted with prehistoric remains and many dramatic

Celtic crosses, such as the high crosses at Ardboe and Donaghmore. Manor houses and fine courts and elegant Georgian county houses are set gracefully in velvety green fields while stone churches and ancient monastic settlements echo a more distant past. Innisfallen Abbey on an island in Lough Leane was founded in the 7th century and was inhabited well into the 1300s while Muckross Abbey in the Killarney National Park, County Kerry, was built in 1448 as a Franciscan friary; its huge yew tree is said to be as old as the abbey itself.

Opposite above: Medieval Dunluce castle, built on the site of an early fort, perches on a headland overlooking the North Antrim coast.

Opposite below: A small whitewashed stone cottage in the old village weathers the storms on tranquil Great Blasket Island.

Below: Set on its rocky spur, mighty Carrickfergus Castle dominates the town and harbor — and has done so since the late 1170s.

Mysterious round towers

The mysterious remains of some 65 fine round towers soar heavenward around the Irish landscape, many within monastery grounds to spike the 'land of saints and scholars.' Possibly they were used as lookout posts or places of refuge during Viking attacks but there is much debate as to their purpose. They are believed to have been built between the 7th and 10th centuries AD. These are atmospheric ancient landmarks and include the round towers of Cashel on its rocky outcrop, Glendalough, set in the cleft of a steep, thickly forested valley, Kilmacduagh found north of Limerick, the tallest at 112ft (34m) that appears to be tilting precariously … and Clonmacnoise at Offaly with Celtic high crosses and early Christian grave slabs in attendance.

Ireland has been scraped by glacial iceflows, molded into hills, mountains, and valleys, bejeweled with gleaming lakes and rivers set amid a soft tapestry of emerald fields and velvety patches of woodland. The eagle owl *(Bubo bubo)* — the world's largest with its near 6.5ft (2m) wingspan — is now reappearing in parts of Ireland. Perhaps if we could fly high with one of them and share the keen vision of its huge bright orange eyes as it swoops over the landscape, we should better appreciate how the craggy shores envelop a sweet green countryside, watered by pearly showers, and in parts made the richer by the sculptured swell of purple mountains and moors.

Above: *Dwarfing Celtic crosses, gravestones, cathedral, and castle, the round tower soars 90ft (28m) high on the Rock of Cashel, seat of the Munster kings. This awesome rocky stronghold was long a seat of power — both priestly and royal.*

Opposite above: *Glendalough has both a monastery and a tall round tower, possibly built to protect the religious treasures from Viking piracy. In more peaceful times, this was a serene retreat established by Saint Kevin in the 6th century.*

Left: *Clonmacnoise in County Offaly is one of Ireland's earliest monastic settlements, some 1500 years old, set on the banks of the River Shannon. Here is an enigmatic mix of Celtic high crosses, cathedral ruins, and ten ancient churches in what was once a medieval city and important seat of learning.*

CHAPTER 3

TOWNS AND VILLAGES

The Emerald Isle is justifiably proud of its fine cities, towns, and villages, many steeped in history and legend. Visitors will encounter twisting streets, old gateways and well-worn steps, and a rich architectural heritage encompassing distinctive mills, distilleries, monasteries, abbeys, castles, forts, harbors, inns, museums, shops, and colleges. Many places have witnessed long centuries of colonization and emigration, battles and conflict, building and growth so that today they reflect the influence of the Celts, Vikings, Normans, and English who have landed in this country — yet all the while retaining their unique Irish spirit.

Above: *Dublin is particularly famous for its fine Georgian architecture.*

Left: *Waterford is a busy maritime city and former shipbuilding center.*

Ireland throngs with communities of all sizes — villages and ports, small towns and busy cities — all bursting with history. However, Ireland is sparsely populated, especially when compared to other European nations with their ever-growing populations. In historical terms, this population decline is a relatively recent trend. The current number of people living in Ireland (slightly over 6 million) is significantly lower now than it was, say, 150 years ago. Some 4,340,000 reside in the Republic of Ireland (of which 1.7 million live in County Dublin) and 1,750,000 in Northern Ireland, where eastern Ulster has Ireland's highest population density after Dublin. Way back in 1841, the population of the entire island was considerably more — some 8,175,124 according to the Census.

Population density

Today the greatest concentrations of people are found around the east and south coasts, with the highest densities being in Belfast, Cork, and Dublin. While the overall number in the north is less, Northern Ireland is more densely populated than the Republic, with its borders encompassing almost one-third of Irish people. A million of them live in Counties Antrim and Down. The area around Belfast Lough is very busy, with the six towns of Bangor, Belfast, Carrickfergus, Lisburn, Newtownabbey, and Newtownards each boasting over 20,000 inhabitants and the Belfast urban area being home to some 276,000 people.

In the Irish Republic, nine towns (Bray, Cork, Drogheda, Dublin, Dundalk, Dún Laoghaire, Galway, Limerick, and Waterford) have over 20,000 inhabitants. One in five Irish people live in County Dublin, where — bucking the trend — numbers have been rising quickly in recent decades, with a 2006 population count of 505,739 people in Dublin city.

A trip across to the west coast offers a very different prospect. Here the sparse population is scattered along the fringes and hinterlands. The best agricultural land lies in Ireland's eastern coastal areas, conveniently close to the potential markets of Britain and the rest of Europe. It was ever so, for this eastern edge was the area settled first by successive waves of invaders: Celts, Vikings, Normans, and English landed here and established first their territorial claims and then their communities.

A rural tradition

Historically, Ireland has maintained a mainly rural culture. It is traditionally a place for fishing (off the coasts and in the lakes) and for farming. This was a land where both the ordinary folk and monks tilled the soil and where the rich oversaw large country estates. Today it is a rather different story: Ireland is becoming increasingly urbanized, especially in Northern Ireland where now over 70 percent of the population live in urban communities housing over a thousand people. Yet, despite these trends toward greater urbanization and industrialization, Ireland still retains its special rural flavor for even the largest towns are set amid beautiful countryside, close to hills, lakes, seascapes, or mountains — and all are steeped in history and legend.

Above: Limerick's modern architecture reflects the Republic of Ireland's dynamic 21st-century role as a thriving industrial nation.

Opposite: There are still beguiling thatched cottages to be found.

Left: The busy O'Connell Bridge over the River Liffey in Dublin.

An A to Z of towns in Northern Ireland

Armagh and Ballycastle

A city with fine Georgian terraces, two cathedrals (Anglican and Roman Catholic), and many orchards planted long ago by 17th-century English settlers, Armagh was named Ard Macha (Macha's Height) after the legendary pagan goddess who built a site for ceremonial ritual on the hill here. In about 445, Saint Patrick arrived to convert Ireland to Christianity and chose Armagh as a center for the new religion; it soon developed into an ecclesiastical capital. The Battle of Yellow Ford on the River Blackwater was fought here in 1598 while, in 1646, some 3000 Scots were killed when their army was outmaneuvered at the Battle of Benburb. Today's less brutal 'battles' in the area include the ancient game of road bowls when a heavy iron ball is hurled along a country road course up to 2.5 miles (4km) long. The player who covers the distance in the fewest throws wins the contest.

Ballycastle in County Antrim is a lovely town set on the sea front, beside the Margy River. Ireland's oldest traditional market fair, The Oul' Lammas Fair, is held here in August when the town becomes a busy focus for horse-trading, competitions, street performers, and market stalls. Here is an attractive small harbor and marina area with a ferry service that takes vehicles across to Rathlin Island. Ballycastle has associations with the radio pioneer Guglielmo Marconi: his mother was Irish (her family owned the Jameson Whiskey Distillery in County Wexford) and, in 1898, Marconi and his assistants sent a radio signal from a lighthouse on Rathlin Island to a house by Ballycastle harbor — possibly the first ever successfully transmitted wireless signal.

Above: Guglielmo Marconi carried out experimental radio transmissions between a lighthouse on Rathlin Island and White Lodge cottage. He and his assistant George Kemp lived here for a brief spell, just 3 miles (5km) from Ballycastle seafront. The first successful signal from Rathlin Island was detected on July 6 1898.

Top: Ballycastle developed around a castle raised by the first Earl of Antrim. Some 18 fairs are held here annually plus a weekly fair; Tuesday has traditionally been market day since about 1612.

Opposite: Armagh's Roman Catholic St Patrick's Cathedral has a split personality! The bottom half was designed in 1838 by Thomas Duff of Newry (in the English Perpendicular style); the top section was designed 15 years later (in the French Decorated Gothic style) by J. J. McCarthy of Dublin.

Belfast

Belfast (County Antrim and County Down) has been the capital of Northern Ireland since 1920. Set by the River Lagan that flows past the south side of the city to Belfast Lough (a finger-shaped inlet), this industrial and predominantly Victorian city was raised on a site that has been occupied since the Bronze Age — Cave Hill was first carved out during Neolithic times. Belfast's recent stormy history during the Troubles brought it much unwelcome attention but the city has been famous far longer for the textile, ropemaking, tobacco, engineering, and shipbuilding industries which boomed here in the 18th and 19th centuries. It was here that the ill-fated RMS *Titanic* was built. The Harland & Wolff shipyard became the largest in the UK. It was named for a Yorkshire engineer, Sir Edward Harland, and Gustav Wolff, a marine draftsman from Hamburg. In its prosperous heyday, the shipyard where the work was undertaken employed more than 30,000 people but now only a small workforce is found here — mainly undertaking ship repair and conversion and supplying equipment for the offshore oil and gas industry.

The city has many narrow alleys alive with atmospheric taverns as well as handsome streets. Attractions here include a fine City Hall with a copper dome, St Anne's Cathedral with gorgeous mosaics, a sumptuous Opera House, lovely botanic gardens, the red and yellow Tudor-style Queen's University, Belfast Castle, and Ulster Museum — home to some treasures from the Spanish Armada ship *Girona* that was shipwrecked near the Giant's Causeway. Belfast's wonderfully ornate Crown Liquor Saloon in Great Victoria Street dates back to the 1880s; those who have a taste for literature rather than Guinness can revel instead in the superb Linen Hall Library. Founded in 1788 it is the oldest library in Belfast. At MacArt's Fort on Cavehill above the city, Wolfe Tone and the United Irishmen pledged to rebel against British rule in 1795.

Above: Belfast City Hall was designed to reflect Belfast's City status, granted by Queen Victoria in 1888. Built in Portland stone, it was completed in 1906. To one side now stands the massive structure of the popular 'Big Wheel' attraction, opened in 2007, which offers spectacular views across the city from a height of 200ft (60m).

Opposite: The Grand Opera House in Belfast has been extensively restored. Its magnificent auditorium is in lavish Oriental style.

Right: Belfast-built RMS Titanic *leaves the city for her sea trials in 1912. She is being guided down Belfast Lough by tugs.*

Above: *From The Queen's Bridge over the Lagan River there is a fine view of Northern Ireland's capital. Belfast (Béal Feirste) means*

Bushmills, Carrickfergus, and Derry

Bushmills sits slightly inland from the north Antrim coastline, not far from the Giant's Causeway. Here a variety of mills worked with flax and corn — and factories produced spades. Undoubtedly the most famous product, however, is the whiskey created in the Old Bushmills Distillery, set on the riverbank. It is the oldest licensed distillery in the world — in operation since 1608. However, Irish whiskey was probably first made at least a thousand years ago by monks who returned from missionary work in Asia.

The medieval town of Carrickfergus was named for the basalt Rock of Fergus, off which King Fergus, who founded the Royal House of Scotland, was supposedly shipwrecked in about AD 320. There is a small sandy beach, a marina, and traces of the old town walls; the north gate has been restored … but the town is best known for the splendid Anglo-Norman

Castle which stands beside the harbor on a basalt rock protruding into the sea (see also page 67). King John laid siege to and slept in the castle in 1210; Edward Bruce seized it after a year-long siege in 1316; and King William landed at the ancient quay here on his way to the Battle of the Boyne. The old County Antrim courthouse was the scene of the 1797

trial of United Irishman William Orr who was eventually hanged despite three postponed executions. Nearby is Kilroot church (founded in AD 412 which predates the mission of St Patrick) where Dean Swift first worked as a clerk in 1695. The family of US President Andrew Jackson came from this area.

Just around the corner from the border and set beside the River Foyle is the old walled city of Derry (Londonderry), Northern Ireland's second largest city. It has an ancient history, launched by Saint Columba's founding a monastery here in 546. There is a wonderful 1633 Gothic cathedral named for him. Derry's ancient city walls — never breached — have four gates: Bishop Gate, Ferryquay Gate, Shipquay Gate, and Butcher Gate. The ruined castle was built by Richard de Burgo, named for his florid complexion as the Red Earl of Ulster. In 1932, aviator Amelia Earhart landed near here after completing the first transatlantic solo flight by a woman.

Background: Carrickfergus is justifiably proud of its splendid castle, one of Ireland's best-preserved medieval structures, dating from 1177 and set on the shore of Belfast Lough, gateway to the Irish Sea.

Enniskillen, Larne, Lisburn, and Lurgan

Enniskillen lies between Upper and Lower Lough Erne, linked by the winding River Erne that splits into two arms to create an island — and the setting for most of the town, that is dominated by Fort Hill with its Cole Tower monument. A site of strategic importance, the town has witnessed many battles. A stone castle was raised here by 1439, now absorbed by the present castle. The region has several ruined fortifications from the plantation period and a 1637 Gothic parish church, now rebuilt as a cathedral. Nearby is sumptuous neoclassical Castle Coole and the Portora Royal School, founded in 1618 and later attended by the future authors Oscar Wilde and Samuel Beckett.

With its name meaning the domain of a Viking chief, Larne on the east coast of County Antrim has been a seaport for a thousand years or more and was a landing place even back in Mesolithic times. Edward Bruce landed Scottish troops in the area in 1315. Later, in the 18th century, many Irish emigrated to America from here and a Curran Park monument commemorates the *Friends Goodwill*, the first emigrant ship to sail from here in 1717 — to Boston. In 1914, when there was great opposition in Ulster to the Home Rule Act, German weapons and ammunition sent secretly were landed at Larne by night and then distributed to Loyalists around the country.

The linen towns

Lisburn, which gained its city status in 2002, is where the Irish linen industry was established in 1698 by Huguenots fleeing religious persecution in France. Negotiations preceding the American War of Independence were conducted nearby when Lord Hillsborough and Benjamin Franklin met at Hillsborough, a pretty Georgian village just to the south. Today Lisburn's Thiepval Barracks (named for a French village that featured in the 1916 Battle of the Somme) are the headquarters of the British Army in Northern Ireland. Set well inland and south of Lough Neagh in County Armagh, Lurgan is another linen-making town from the late 1600s. It has straight wide streets, rows of cottages, and Northern Ireland's biggest urban park with a fine lake and beautiful Elizabethan Brownlow House.

Above left: An illuminated tree stands before Lisburn's Island Art Center, an impressive contemporary workshop and exhibition venue.

Left: A traditional loom at the Irish Linen Center in Lisburn.

Opposite: Chain Tower Lighthouse at the entrance to Larne Lough.

Newcastle, Newry, and Newtownbutler

South of Belfast City, in the shadow of the Mourne Mountains, lies Newcastle, a seaside resort with a promenade and fine sweeping golden beach. To the north lies the Leganamny dolmen which is thought to be more than 4000 years old, while to the south is a harbor, the stump of a round tower and a ruined church. Nearby are Donard Cave, a cliff ravine called Maggie's Leap and, at Ballyvaston, a complete village buried in the sands — it was only rediscovered in 1735 when a great storm uncovered some of the remains.

The town, garrison, and port of Newry nestle between the scenic Mourne Mountains and the Ring of Gullion at the head of Carlingford Lough, close to the north-south border. Newry was named for a yew tree, said to have been planted by

Above: Houses crowd along the seashore at Newcastle (County Down) where the Royal County Down golf course is said to be one of the best in the world. It is a favorite of Tiger Woods.

Below: The ancient yew trees at Crom predate the present castle by several centuries. Near the ruins of old Crom Castle, parties of 200 people are said to have dined beneath the vast yews that once measured about 75ft (23m) across.

Saint Patrick in the 5th century. This thriving town is one of Northern Ireland's oldest, founded in 1144, with a monastery raised in 1157 by Maurice McLoughlin, King of Ireland — both yew tree and monastery were burned down in 1162. A castle was built by John de Courcy, burned by Edward Bruce in 1315, rebuilt, and then destroyed again. After its dissolution, the monastery and lands were granted to one Nicholas Bagenal who developed the town — colonizing it, rebuilding the castle, and raising the parish church of St Patrick, possibly Ireland's earliest Protestant place of worship. The first Irish mail coach, linking Belfast and Dublin in 1790, is said to have been established by a Newry firm. Today several Georgian houses are found here as well as local shops, and a canal busy with waterfowl and criss-crossing bridges.

Newtownbutler in County Fermanagh (Ireland's Lake District) was a 17th-century plantation village originally called Newtown and renamed Newtownbutler when Theophilus Butler was created a baron of the area in 1715. It was the scene of a battle in 1689 when a Williamite force of just 1000 Enniskillen troops captured and killed 3000 Jacobite soldiers here, somewhat assisted by the fact that James's men stumbled into a treacherous bog. Nearby is Crom — with Northern Ireland's largest surviving oak woodlands, which support populations of purple hair-streak and wood white butterflies, red squirrels, otters, fallow deer, Irish hares, eight species of bats, and pine martens. Here too is Ireland's largest heronry, plus 19th-century neo-Tudor Crom Castle with its magnificent vast yew trees, reputed to be over 800 years old.

Omagh and Warrenpoint

Omagh, the county town of County Tyrone, was founded as a town in 1610, but there was a Franciscan friary here a century and a half before that and an abbey was founded even earlier in 792, making this one of Ireland's oldest towns. Today, sadly, the associations are also with the sectarian violence and bombing outrage of 1998 in which 29 people were killed. Omagh is also known as having been a safe haven for fugitives during the 1641 Rebellion and for the 1995 discovery of deposits of silver and gold in the bogland here. The countryside surrounding Omagh and Warrenpoint is beautiful — a place where sheep peacefully graze while beyond the farms, small villages, and emerald fields rise the dramatic Sperrin Mountains.

Warrenpoint was originally a small quiet place with a school and courthouse, enlivened by regular fairs and markets. Then in the mid-19th century local merchants had a tidal dock built, and the Newry, Warrenpoint and Rostrevor Railway soon followed. In 1849, the passenger ferry to Omeath in the Irish Republic began services and it is still operating today in summer. There are early 20th-century swimming baths here and a bandstand in the park. Nearby is a 1560 tower house, Old Narrow Water Castle, a three-story tower house built to protect the entrance to Newry River.

Above: Children wait for a tram in Rostrevor. From 1877, horse-drawn trams ran from Warrenpoint Railway Station to the Great Northern Hotel, providing local transport until later replaced by buses.

Left: Near Omagh rise the rugged Sperrins — capped with crystalline limestone and often dusted even whiter with winter snow.

An A to Z of towns in the Republic of Ireland

Adare and Ardmore

Adare (County Limerick) is sometimes called the prettiest village in Ireland with many picturesque thatched cottages as well as stone buildings, medieval churches, and romantic ruins — all in a woodland setting. It was not always so peaceful: wars and rebellions have been fought hereabouts and the old town on the northern riverbank, near Desmond Castle, was destroyed during 14th-century battles. Most of the present village was built in the 1800s.

Set on the coast between Waterford and Cork, Ardmore offers the chance to see the very atmospheric Ardmore Cathedral (built on the site of St Declan's Monastery) with its wonderful Romanesque sculptures and ruins dwarfed by the adjacent 12th-century round tower. The nearby oratory may well mark the site of the saint's grave.

Above: At Ardmore the ancient and highly decorative ruins of St Declan's are set next to a tapering round tower that dates from the 12th century. The church is named for a bishop who lived in the region during the period AD 350-450 and founded a monastery here before Saint Patrick even arrived … so this may be the oldest Christian settlement in Ireland.

Opposite: The colorful thatched cottages in Adare are bright with flowers. This pretty village, set beside the River Maigue, also boasts Tudor-style houses, beautiful gardens, fascinating churches, a Heritage Center, Gothic-revival Adare Manor with its French-style gardens, and a fine medieval fortified castle.

Birr, Blarney, and Boyle

Birr (in County Offaly) in the center of Ireland is the setting for the Birr stone that some claim to be a candidate for the *Umbilicus Hiberniae* (Navel of Ireland), marking the country's central point. Here too are superb colorful old shop fronts and Gothic Birr Castle, surrounded by magnificent gardens and parkland; here, over the last 400 years, the Parsons family have contributed to the advancement of botany, astronomy, photography, and engineering. They are justifiably proud of the great Leviathan of Parsonstown, an astronomical telescope with a 72-inch reflector mirror that was, until 1917, the world's largest.

Kissing the Blarney Stone

Northwest of Cork City, the village folk of Blarney (County Cork) gather in its square, a flat grassy area enclosed by a waist-high perimeter wall. The architecture here is mostly Tudor in style but visitors are generally more anxious to flock to the famous castle (see also page 120). This was built on a sheer rock cliff and its mighty battlements have set into them the famous Blarney Stone. The grounds have interesting rock formations, such as the witch's kitchen and wishing steps, a

hermit's cave, an ancient sacrificial altar, a druid's circle, and dolmen. Here too are fairy glades and sturdy old yew trees plus a little meandering stream, glittering with coins tossed in by visitors as they have crossed over the little bridges. Many tourists also visit the 19th-century traditional wool-weaving factory of Blarney Mills.

Boyle (County Roscommon) has an elegant Palladian mansion, King House, built around 1730 by Sir Henry King, a member of a wealthy and powerful local family. There is also beautiful Cistercian Boyle Abbey, founded in 1161 and later converted into a castle — but still retaining its cloisters, cellars, and kitchen.

Above: Birr Castle, home to the Seventh Earl of Rosse, boasts an enormous telescope and 300-year-old box hedges which The Guinness Book of Records *claims are the tallest in the world.*

Opposite: In about 1210 a stone castle replaced a 10th-century wooden castle at Blarney. The present keep dates from 1446 when this third castle was built by Dermot McCarthy, King of Munster.

Cahir, Cashel, and Cork

Cahir in County Tipperary was once a garrison and milltown. Today, the main attraction is the formidable castle, set on a rocky island in the River Suir and dating from the 1200s; it was used as a location for the movie *Excalibur* in 1981. Here too is the delightful Swiss Cottage folly designed by Regency architect John Nash with its decorative timberwork and sloping eaves.

From the 4th or 5th century, Cashel (County Tipperary) was the seat of the kings of Munster and it was here that an Irish king was converted to Christianity by Saint Patrick in the 400s. Under the protection of the dramatic Rock of Cashel, a cluster of ancient monuments rise dramatically from the surrounding plain. Here are found ancient city walls, buildings from the 1100s and 1200s, a 12th-century round tower soaring up to 92ft (28m), the Romanesque King Cormac's Chapel (consecrated 1134), Gothic 13th-century St Patrick's Cathedral, and enigmatic high crosses. A plethora of places to visit include the Cistercian Hoare Abbey with its fascinating graveyard, the 15th-century castle, an austere Dominican Friary, and Cashel Folk Village … while the Brú Ború Heritage Center here has a model of Cashel in the 1640s as well as the charters of Charles II (1663) and James II (1687). Cashel encompasses an amazing concentration of medieval art and architecture in a stunning setting.

Built on a marsh

Set on the River Lee and with one of the world's finest natural deep-water harbors, Cork is Ireland's third largest city (after Dublin and Belfast). The name Cork comes from the Irish term *Corcaigh* meaning marsh and, indeed, the town rose on an island in the swampy river estuary, with many of the streets being built on former river channels and canals. In the 12th century Viking pirates raided and burned the early town but then returned to settle and trade. Both the Danish lords and local McCarthy chiefs were forced to submit to English King Henry II after the Anglo-Norman invasion in 1172 and the city was granted its first city charter by King John in 1185. But its population always displayed an independent streak and the town was long known for its stubborn rebels.

Many of Cork's old gateways and steps once led to boathouses and warehouses, serving busy merchants who negotiated the waterways. The hilly streets corkscrew up and down and around; to find their bearings, many visitors climb up to Elizabeth Fort where they can enjoy an excellent panoramic view over Cork. Alternatively, a trip to Cork City Gaol, just outside the city center, provides a good viewpoint as well as the chance to see the cells and a human treadmill.

Other city sights include St Fin Barre's Cathedral, a 19th-century building erected on a holy site dating back to the 7th century and dedicated to Cork's patron saint, who founded the original monastery here; the Butter Exchange in the Shandon area from where 500,000 casks of butter were once despatched across the world each year; and the steeple of the Church of St Anne with its renowned bells and salmon-shaped weather vane; a National Monument commemorates the 1798 and 1867 uprising and rebels. Everywhere there are colorful shops, pubs, and markets with lively music adding to the bohemian flavor. Cork revels in the arts during its midsummer festival featuring theater, music, poetry—and film and jazz festivals in October.

Above: Cahir is a vibrant market town set beside the River Suir at the foot of the Galtee Mountains. Long ago this was a defense town and it was also one the first hereabouts to have a stagecoach service in the 19th century.

Top: Hoare Abbey is a ruined Cistercian monastery. Behind rises the spectacular Rock of Cashel — the traditional seat of the Kings of Munster for centuries. On the hilltop plateau, walls enclose a castle, a round tower, the Chapel of King Cormac, a 13th-century cathedral, and a number of superb high crosses.

Left: The very attractive Swiss Cottage near Cahir was built in about 1810 for the last Earl of Glengall and was probably designed by renowned Regency architect, John Nash.

Above: *Cork City Hall (opened 1936) is the headquarters for the city's administration. The building includes a fine concert hall. Its six limestone Tuscan pillars and copper-domed clock tower look very elegant, especially when illuminated at night.*

Right: *The origins of the English market date back to the reign of King James I but the present market building was raised in 1786. Stalls here offer a good range of fish, fruit, meat, vegetables, and bread.*

Opposite: *Cork sits on an island between two channels of the River Lee. Beside the triple-spired St Fin Barre's Cathedral, higgledy-piggledy buildings, gates, alleyways, and old quays crowd busy riverbanks, linked by many bridges.*

Dingle, Doolin, Donegal, and Drogheda

The first two of these small towns are both known for their traditional Irish music. County Kerry's Dingle is set by a natural harbor below Slievanea mountain, sheltered by hills on three sides, on the beautiful Dingle peninsula (see also page 44). It is well known for the friendliness of its people, restaurants, pubs and the bottlenose dolphin that visits the lovely little harbor.

A little farther north is Doolin (County Clare), a small fishing village with a rich heritage of traditional music, singing, dancing, and story-telling. There are three renowned pubs where live music can be heard (McGanns, O'Connor's, and McDermott's), as well as several Iron Age sites and fine castles nearby.

Overshadowed by the Bluestack Mountains, Donegal in County Donegal was once a Norse settlement with a Viking fortress. Many other even more ancient roundworks and earthworks can also be found here. It also boasts a castle (incorporating a 15th-century fortified manor house) and a Franciscan abbey south of a market square called the Diamond. The town was once home to the O'Donnell clan who from the 15th to the 17th century strongly opposed English colonization of Ireland. The Irish Famine hit hard here as the records of the workhouse (now part of the hospital) and a famine grave show.

History and romance

Drogheda, in County Louth, north of Dublin, was a trading post from Roman times and grew to become one of Ireland's most important towns, set in a prime position near the mouth of the River Boyne and fortified with a Norman motte crowned by a Martello tower. Today it is most notoriously remembered for the trauma of the 1649 Siege of Drogheda when Cromwell's forces captured the town from its Royalist defenders and killed some 2000 of the garrison's armed troops as well as hundreds of civilian townspeople.

The embalmed head of saint and martyr Archbishop Oliver Plunkett (hanged, drawn, and quartered at Tyburn, London, in 1681 for his alleged complicity in the Popish Plot) can be seen in Drogheda's Catholic St Peter's Church. Canonized in 1975, he became the first new Irish saint for almost seven centuries. Today, more happily, samba bands from around the world gather here for a week of drumming and parades each summer. Just to the west of the town lies Ireland's first Cistercian monastery, Mellifont Abbey, founded in 1142, now a romantic ruin but with fragments of beautiful Romanesque cloisters still in evidence on the site.

Above: Donegal Castle is a restored Jacobean mansion developed from a 15th-century tower house on the Eske riverbank.

Top: Mellifont Abbey, set in a tranquil valley, was Ireland's first Cistercian abbey. After its foundation in 1142 Cistercian communities spread throughout the land.

Opposite: Peaceful Fisher Street in Doolin (now featured as a Netherworld portal in the Playstation game Folklore). Around the bay, overlooking the isles of Aran, is Doonagore Castle (below).

These pages: A market town and fishing port, Dingle is the most westerly town in Ireland. In medieval times pilgrims embarked from here on voyages to Spain and the grave of St James at Santiago de Compostela. Today Dingle is justifiably renowned as an excellent tourist center. It has beautiful scenery all around, colorful houses, excellent restaurants, fine galleries, shops selling virtually everything — from local crafts to Wellington boots, beds, and bicycles — and live music in many vibrant pubs. When it rains here, the locals accommodatingly say it's a 'soft day,' but the sun usually shines through again to turn the boat-bobbing sea azure blue once more.

Dublin

Ireland's capital is a vibrant city, full of lively pubs, a multitude of fascinating museums, gorgeous green parks (including vast Phoenix Park and lovely St Stephen's Green), and beautiful buildings — many fine ones standing beside the River Liffey. The city derived its name from Dubh Linn, a 'dark pool' where the rivers Poddle and Liffey converge. Back in the 9th century, Vikings established the first permanent settlement here beside the Liffey at Wood Quay, where excavations have revealed the remains of 150 Viking buildings. (However, there is evidence that human settlement in the area dates back much farther than that.) The Norsemen held on with great tenacity until, in 1014, at the Battle of Clontarf on the shore of Dublin Bay, BrianBorú managed to curb their power, although he was killed in the fight.

Dublin's history from its earliest times — including the impact of the Vikings, the medieval Corn Market, Georgian developments, the valor and horror of the 1916 Easter Rising and then the signing of the Anglo-Irish Treaty in 1921 — can all be explored in Dublin's National Museum. It contains over 2,000,000 artefacts including the gorgeous 8th-century Tara brooch and a beautiful miniature golden boat from the 1st century AD.

There is so much to see and discover in this city — the port area straddling the estuary on the shores of Dublin Bay; Dublin Castle; the magnificent Book of Kells in elegant Trinity College; gabled 17th-century houses built by French Huguenots; sweeping Georgian terraces and neoclassical buildings raised during the period of 18th-century prosperity; the amazing story of the Guinness brewery; Fishamble Street, where Molly Malone reputedly was born and where the first performance of Handel's *Messiah* was given; and information

about authors such as Jonathan Swift, W.B. Yeats, Oscar Wilde, and George Bernard Shaw in the Dublin Writers Museum. Statues in the city depict Dublin's famous personalities including Molly Malone (called by the local wits *The Dish with the Fish*), James Joyce *(The Crank on the Bank)* while the personification of the River Liffey, Anna Livia, is unceremoniously referred to as *The Floozie in the Jacuzzi*!

Above: *The Custom House in Dublin rises in an elegant flourish beside the River Liffey, which reflects the building's beautifully proportioned façade, richly adorned with sculptures and coats of arms.*

Opposite: *A castle has stood on this site since the days of King John but the present structure of Dublin Castle, once a fortified seat of British rule, dates from the 18th century and is now used for state functions.*

Above left: In 1790 the Irish Parliament granted funds to the Dublin Society to establish a public botanic garden — ultimately founded in 1795 on lands at Glasnevin — with the advancement of botanical knowledge a major aim. It was curator David Moore who first noted potato blight at Glasnevin in August 1845 and correctly predicted that its impact on the crop would lead to famine.

Above right: Dublin's Trinity College is an ancient, prestigious university, founded in 1592 by Queen Elizabeth I. Graduates have included Samuel Beckett, Bram Stoker, Jonathan Swift, Oscar Wilde, and three Irish presidents. Ireland's oldest surviving harp and the famous Book of Kells are in the beautiful library here where four million volumes include 200,000 antiquarian texts, manuscripts, maps, and music.

Left: The 1987 statue of Molly Malone by Dublin-born sculptor Jeanne Rynhart stands at the top of Grafton Street and was inspired by the popular song of the same name (albeit sometimes called 'Cockles and Mussels'). Locals refer affectionately to the statue as 'The Dish with the Fish'!

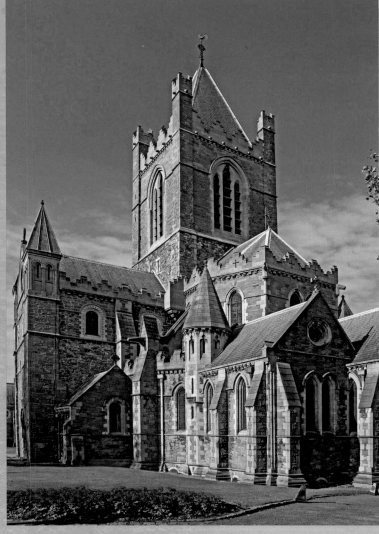

Medieval streets

If the excitement and bustle of the lovely lively city of Dublin should prove too much, it is easy to escape to sandy beaches nearby and the Wicklow Mountains rising above lush green valleys. Just south of Dublin on the tip of Dublin Bay is charming little Dalkey with its medieval streets, villas, and a rocky island offshore that is a bird sanctuary. It was here that James Joyce set one chapter of *Ulysses*, and it also features prominently in the work of the writer Flann O'Brien. Present-day writers living near here include Maeve Binchy.

Above right: Christ Church Cathedral, Dublin. The first wooden church here was built in 1038 by Viking king, Sitric Silkenbeard. In 1171 it was extended and rebuilt in stone by Norman baron, Richard de Clare, but it was King Henry VIII who converted the priory into a cathedral in the midst of the city in 1539.

Left: Goats, rabbits, and walkers roam Dalkey Island as fishermen and divers explore the coastal resources of what was once a Viking base. There is a ruined church, Martello tower, and gun battery.

Above: The shallow-domed Dublin Four Courts (named for four judicial divisions — Chancery, King's Bench, Exchequer, and Common Pleas) look especially splendid at night, gleaming beside the Liffey.

Top: Grafton Street, here bright with Christmas decorations, is nearly always busy with shoppers, buskers, visitors, and friends meeting at its bustling restaurants and cafes.

Left: The Ha'penny Bridge over Dublin's River Liffey opened in 1816 when it was officially called Wellington Bridge after the Iron Duke. Its new colloquial name arose from the one old halfpenny toll that had to be paid to cross what was the only pedestrian bridge over the river until the new Millennium Bridge opened in 2000.

Dundalk, Ennis, and Galway

The crest for Dundalk (County Louth) reads *The place where brave Cúchulainn was born*, remembering the young mythical warrior — the Irish equivalent of the Greek hero, Heracles — who defended Ulster single-handedly against the armies of Queen Medb of Connacht. The town developed from prehistoric origins through Celtic, Christian, and Norman settlement to become a medieval hub but, in the 17th century, Lord Limerick created a 'modern' town with fine streets leading to its center and connecting with a new Market Square — and this is what still survives. Soon there were linen factories, more industry developed and, in due course, railway connections and busy docks were established.

Ennis (County Clare), on the River Fergus, is rather less industrial and is known for its ruined friary (established around 1240), music festivals, fun 'singing' pubs, and the Queen's Hotel that featured in James Joyce's *Ulysses*. Here are narrow streets with pretty painted shop fronts, a thriving market square, cobble-stoned courtyard, and renowned restaurants — fine chefs arrived here in the 1950s to cook for the airline crews landing at nearby Shannon airport.

Steeped in history

Lovely Galway, the county town and university city at the mouth of the Corrib River in the west of Ireland (where the mild, moist climate encourages palm and fig trees to flourish) exults in a riot of summer festivals celebrating Irish music, food, and culture with a traditional Oyster Festival in September. Both pubs and streets ooze music. The port boasts original old quays and the Spanish Arch where once galleons unloaded goods; newer docks now extend into Lough Atalia. Galway developed from Anglo-Norman origins into a medieval settlement with walls and towers, controlled by 14 merchant families. It still has narrow winding streets, now lined with colorful shops and restaurants. The town was captured by the forces of William of Orange in the 1690s; the great families were ruined and Galway did not fully recover until the economic boom regenerated its fortunes three centuries later. Eyre Square was renamed the Kennedy Memorial Park to honor President John F. Kennedy, who visited Galway just before his assassination in 1963.

Opposite: The ruins of Ennis Friary — once home to some 300 Franciscan friars and 600 students. It was established in 1240 and became an important center of learning, renowned throughout Europe, with dormitories, workshops, cloisters, and a vast kitchen.

Above: Ennis, the county town of Clare (top), developed around a thriving friary, with narrow streets dating back to medieval times. By contrast Galway grew up around an ancient fort. Its City Museum and Spanish Arch (center) are a popular tourist destination as is the busy harbor (above).

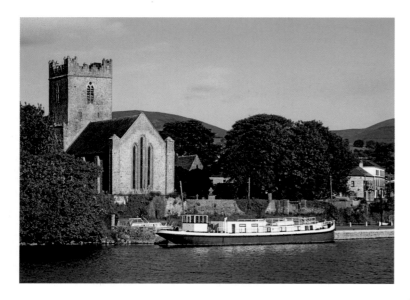

Kildare, Kilkenny, and Killaloe

Ancient Kildare was the site of a shrine to Celtic goddess Brigid and it was a Christian Saint Brigid who in 480 founded an abbey for both monks and nuns — where the present cathedral now stands. Until the Reformation in 1540 a perpetual fire was maintained here in Saint Brigid's memory; the fire pit (and a round tower) are still in evidence. Today, Kildare is home to some of the world's finest thoroughbreds with the Irish National Stud being based here as are many other horse breeding centers. The Curragh racecourse is found nearby. There are also beautiful gardens including the enchanting Japanese Gardens and St Fiachra's Garden laid out 1906-10.

Kilkenny is famous for brewing, the sport of hurling, and as Confederate Ireland's former capital between 1642 and 1649. Many fine old medieval buildings remain and it is sometimes called the Marble City on account of the renowned local black stone. The skyline is dominated by the wonderful Norman castle and St Canice's Cathedral, set beside a fine round tower. Here are vibrant pubs and nightlife where everyone enjoys the *craic*, with Kyteler's Inn being famous for its original owner, Dame Alice le Kyteler, who was burned at the stake for witchcraft in the 14th century. Festivals celebrate hot-air balloons, art, and music while annual concerts have seen Rod Stewart, Bob Dylan, Paul Simon, and Andrea Bocelli perform here. Comedy festivals have earned Kilkenny the title of Comedy Capital of the World. In earlier times writer Jonathan Swift and philosopher George Berkeley attended Kilkenny College (founded 1538).

Killaloe (County Clare) has a majestic arched bridge over the River Shannon linking it with Ballina, a 13th-century cathedral, and a network of charming narrow streets, flanked by old shops and houses scrambling up a steep hill. It is a busy fishing and boating center. This was the birthplace of Brian Ború (910–1014), High King of Ireland, marked by an exhibition in a converted boathouse, and there is an annual festival in his honor at the end of June/early July.

Above: The towns of Killaloe (shown here) and Ballina, joined by a 13-arch stone bridge, share a beautiful Shannon riverside setting.

Center: Colorful shop fascia signs and busy pubs and restaurants add visual interest to the streets in Kilkenny.

Top left: Richard de Clare built a Norman tower in Kilkenny in 1172. Today's castle was remodeled in 1661 and 1766. The Butler family lived here for nearly six centuries, from 1391 to 1935.

Opposite: Saint Brigid of Kildare depicted in a stained-glass window.

Kinsale, Kinvara, and Knock

Kinsale (County Cork) is a picturesque resort (see also page 37). The estuary and harbor at the mouth of the River Bandon offer safe anchorage in stormy weather while the town is a maze of narrow streets with many restaurants: some call Kinsale 'Ireland's fine food capital.' Spanish and Irish forces fought the English armies here at the Battle of Kinsale in 1601, a defeat that lead to the evaporation of Spanish help and undermined Irish resistance. Sights include 12th-century St Multose Church and the old courthouse, while Desmond

Castle served as a custom house, a prison for captured French sailors (tragically, a fire in 1747 killed 54 of them), a borough jail, and a workhouse to help the hungry during the Great Famine. It now houses the International Museum of Wine. Charles Fort, a 17th-century star-shaped fort, dominates the entry to Kinsale harbor along with the companion James Fort across the harbor mouth.

Kinvara in County Galway developed around a tower house near the site of the home of a 7th-century king. Ireland's biggest underground river pours into the bay beside Dunguaire

Above: Knock church, 1890 — a crowd gathers, each person hoping for a cure or to witness another miracle. The Virgin Mary, Saint Joseph, and Saint John are said to have appeared on the gable wall in a cloud of light on August 21 1879.

Left: Dunguaire Castle, Kinvara (County Galway) is a well-restored 16th-century tower house in a most romantic setting beside the ocean. It became a meeting place for leading Celtic Revival enthusiasts including Oliver St John Gogarty, Lady Gregory, George Bernard Shaw, John Millington Synge, and W. B. Yeats.

Castle where bards and balladeers once serenaded their king; harpists still play today in its banqueting hall at recreations of medieval banquets. Once a thriving port from where large shipments of corn and seaweed were exported, today the village of fishermen's cottages revels in its May *Cuckoo Festival* of music and August's *Gathering of the Boats*, when traditional sailing craft race one another (they used to transport turf, barley, lime, and timber). The first shots of the 1916 Easter Rising were fired in Kinvara when the Royal Irish Constabulary (RIC) attempted to arrest the local curate.

Every year, some one and a half million pilgrims visit the shrine to the Virgin Mary at Knock (County Mayo). It all began in August 1879 when a vision of the Virgin Mary, Saint Joseph, Saint John the Evangelist and the Lamb of God appeared at the south gable of Knock Parish Church — an apparition that lasted for up to two hours and was witnessed by 15 people ranging from 5 to 75 years of age. Knock soon became an important holy site for Catholic pilgrimage. Pope John Paul II joined the centenary celebrations here in 1979 and Mother Teresa of Calcutta visited the shrine in 1993.

Above: Vessels gather in the almost land-locked natural harbor of Kinsale on the Bandon River estuary. This is a traditional port that caters for both commercial and pleasure craft.

Right: The buildings appear to tumble down the Kinsale hillside to the seashore. Boats were the dominant form of transport here until the 18th century.

Opposite: Kinsale is a delight; its colorful flower-decked buildings seem to pose for the camera in a maze of busy narrow streets, never far from the water.

Background: *Lismore Castle was originally built by King John in the 13th century, who later handed it over to the church. It remained a Bishop's Palace until 1589 when it was acquired by Sir Walter Raleigh and then sold on to Richard Boyle, first Earl of Cork, in 1602.*

Opposite: *King John's Castle in Limerick, set beside the River Shannon on King's Island, was built upon a Viking settlement.*

Limerick, Lismore, and O'Brien's Bridge

Limerick is essentially a medieval city that rose beside the River Shannon where the Vikings landed in 812. It has a cathedral, King John's Castle … and a well-known rugby team! During the 17th century the city was besieged by Cromwell in 1651 and twice by the supporters of William of Orange in the 1690s. However, by the late 18th century, trade had brought riches to Limerick. Today it is famous for the Hunt Museum in the former custom house with works of art that include pieces by Renoir, Picasso, and a bronze horse reputedly from a cast by Leonardo da Vinci. Limerick was the setting for *Angela's Ashes*, the memoir of a young child growing up in poverty, by Frank McCourt. The connection of limerick verse with the city remains obscure.

Today the town of Lismore (County Waterford) is dwarfed by the castle set high above the River Blackwater but its story begins with the arrival of Saint Carthage in AD 636 and the monastery he founded then. Later, in 1627, Robert Boyle was born in the castle here — he was a natural philosopher, chemist, physicist, inventor, the 'Father of Modern Chemistry,' and formulator of Boyle's Law, which states that the pressure and volume of a gas are inversely proportional.

12-arch bridge

Situated on the west side of the River Shannon, O'Brien's Bridge (Galway) is a small village with one main street and a bridge over the river. The first wooden structure was built in 1506 by descendants of Brian Ború but was burned to the ground in 1510 during a war between provincial kings. A new stone Great Bridge with towers and 12ft (3.6m) thick walls rose in its place until a 1537 rebellion against Henry VIII led to an attack on the bridge by the Lord Deputy, Leonard Gray, and its utter destruction after a seven-day battle. Soon, however, a new stone 12-arch bridge, built by one of the O'Briens, once again spanned the river. Eventually the village that grew up around it assumed its name.

Roscommon and Roscrea

The county town of Roscommon, named for Saint Coman who built a monastery here in the 5th century, has a 1269 Anglo-Norman fortress and a 1253 Dominican friary founded by Felim O'Connor, King of Connacht. However, it is also well known for its gaol and last executioner, Lady Betty, who was herself tried in 1780 for the murder of her son but was able to evade punishment by becoming a hangwoman instead, a role in which she served for 30 years.

Like many old Irish towns, Roscrea in County Tipperary first developed around its monastery, a door from which survives in the round tower here. Its beautiful 8th-century *Book of Dimma* — a pocket Gospel enclosed in a bronze shrine with silver plates and Celtic interlacing — is now in Dublin's Trinity College. St Cronan's parish church stands on the site of the ancient monastery while a Catholic church rose on the site of the old Franciscan friary, founded by a local chieftain in 1490. A round tower and some wall sections are what remain of a castle built here by King John; the present Roscrea Castle includes 18th-century Damer House — an elegant residence with a glorious staircase.

Right: This stunning sculpture by Maurice Harron of a Gaelic chieftain on a gleaming horse overlooks Curlew Pass in County Roscommon. Roscommon is a thriving town in Ireland's heartland; its name derives from Ros (meaning a wooded or pleasant gentle height) and Coman, a famous Irish saint.

Slane and Sligo

Rising on a steep hillside is 5000-year-old Slane (County Meath) with a 14th-century bridge, Georgian square, and many 18th-century limestone buildings with oriel windows, stone steps, and archways. The Hill of Slane — visible from the Hill of Tara some 10 miles (16km) away — was in ancient times a site for royal burials, a pagan shrine, and then a Christian abbey. The ruins of the friary church and college have survived here, along with the remains of a 12th-century Norman motte and bailey. The present Slane Castle, with its ancient healing well, stands beside the River Boyne. Once boats sailed to and fro along the river and canals, carrying flour from Ireland's largest flour mill (completed 1766).

Sligo, the county town, has a long history — it was plundered by the Vikings in 807, seized by the Normans in the 11th century and then granted to Maurice Fitzgerald, the Lord Chief Justice of Ireland, who raised both a castle and an abbey here. The O'Conors and O'Donnells fought for ownership for some two centuries and then Cromwell's troops arrived and built a fort. During the 18th century, this busy trading post witnessed many emigrants setting sail for the Americas. Set on the west coast, where the River Garavogue splashes over rocks and ledges to reach the estuary, the market town lies between limestone hills and Lough Gill, amid beautiful scenery. The natural beauty is reflected in the poetry of W.B. Yeats, who spent his childhood here with his brother, artist J.B. Yeats. His famous poem '*The Lake Isle of Innisfree*' was inspired by a small island in Lough Gill nearby.

Above: W.B. Yeats grew up in County Sligo and spent many a summer gazing at the Isle of Innisfree. Homesick in London in the 1880s, he wrote 'The Lake Isle of Innisfree,' remembering the peace and lapping waters of Lough Gill. 'The Isle of Innisfree' was also an immensely popular song recorded by Bing Crosby and used as theme music for the movie, 'The Quiet Man.'

Above: Parke's Castle (County Sligo) is a well-restored, fortified 17th-century manor house set beside Lough Gill's eastern shore. It has a large enclosed courtyard, arches, and turrets and was the home of Robert Parke. Sir Brian O'Rourke, executed at Tyburn in London in 1591, owned an earlier 16th-century tower house here.

Tipperary and Trim

The name Tipperary (County Tipperary) has long been familiar because of the World War One soldiers' marching song, '*It's a long way to Tipperary*' — the large British military barracks here served as a military hospital then. Set among breathtakingly beautiful scenery, the town's origins stretch back to medieval times and it was a busy center of population by the time of King John, but all the ancient fortifications have long vanished.

Trim (County Meath) is a small historic town with 5th-century origins — once an ecclesiastical center on the banks of the River Boyne. Its many ancient ruins include the Echo Gate, where an echo can be heard reflected back across the river, 'Our Lady of Trim' memorial marking a medieval pilgrimage site, St Peter and Paul's Cathedral (which was the largest Gothic church in Ireland) and part of a Hospitaller house. Massive Trim Castle, once the center of feudal power for the de Lacy family, is Ireland's largest Anglo-Norman castle. It has a tall keep, vast thick walls, a heavy gatehouse and deep cellars. Later, the family of the First Duke of Wellington, Arthur Wellesley, owned much of the town. A large part of the movie *Braveheart* was filmed at the castle in the mid-1990s.

Above: The main street of Tipperary in the 1910s; today road signs welcome visitors by saying, 'You've come a long way,' referring to the famous marching song by Harry Williams and Jack Judge.

Top: Tipperary has an ancient history, with several Neolithic sites. It was the first Irish county to be established — in the 13th century. This grand old ruined house reeks of former glories.

Above: The Loughcrew site near Oldcastle town some 20 miles (30km) from Trim, comprises the second largest megalithic cemetery in Ireland, built around 3300 BC with passage tombs and impressive rock carvings. Saint Oliver Plunkett is thought to have been born in a house in the southeast corner of Loughcrew churchyard in 1629.

Right: Trim Castle, constructed over a 30-year period, was an important center of Norman administration. Its massive three-story keep was built in the 1170s on the site of an earlier wooden fortress. The 20-cornered cruciform Great Tower was protected by a ditch, curtain wall, and moat.

Waterford, Westport, and Wexford

Founded by Vikings in AD 914, Waterford is Ireland's oldest city. It is set on the River Suir estuary and was called *Vedrarfjord* (windy fjord) by the Norsemen. It served as a major port for over a millennium. Ancient city walls and a watchtower can still be seen while the Anglo-Norman Reginald's Tower rose on the Viking fort by the long quay. It is Ireland's oldest civic urban building standing at the apex of a triangle of 10th-century fortifications. Waterford is world-famous for its crystal glass factory, originally founded in 1783; here skilled glassblowers still create superb lead crystal pieces and chandeliers but in a new 1947-built factory. The medieval town included the 13th-century Grey Friars. The Georgian Christ Church Cathedral houses a gruesome 15th-century effigy of a rotting corpse while Holy Trinity Church has a rich neoclassical interior.

Westport, a charming town situated on the shores of Clew Bay in County Mayo, is unusual in that it was a planned town, laid out by English architect James Wyatt in 1780. It features elegant tree-lined Georgian streets, notably the beautiful tree-lined boulevard The Mall. The town suffered badly during the Great Famine but remains a gracious place, proud of The Mall and stately Westport House with its marble staircase … and dungeons left over from its predecessor on the site — an O'Malley castle.

Viking town

Wexford was founded by the Vikings in about AD 800 at the mouth of the River Slaney. Today's town with its picturesque narrow cobbled streets and quaint pubs rose on the original Viking fishbone plan. At Selskar Abbey, just outside the town gateway, King Henry II may have done penance for ordering the 1170 murder of Thomas à Becket. During the Middle Ages, Wexford was an Old English settlement and it is

Top left: Set on the banks of the River Suir, with its marina at the heart of a city dating back to Viking times, Waterford hosted the Tall Ships Race in 2005.

Center left: Waterford attracts visitors from around the world and is home to the crystal factory, famous for its elegant fine glassware.

Left: Set on a 125-hectare island, Waterford Castle rose on the site of a Danish camp, monastic settlement, and Norman keep. In the 1700s, socialite Mary Frances Fitzgerald used to be rowed home across the river in a barge, serenaded by 24 musicians.

rumored that Mary Seymour — daughter of Henry VIII's widow, Catherine Parr — was raised here by a family engaged in piracy off the Irish coast while protected by the child's father, Thomas Seymour, an English baron. The town was sacked and burned by Cromwell's troops in 1649 and many inhabitants were massacred in the square, the Bullring, where bulls had been baited in Norman times.

The 1798 rebellion against English rule also saw large numbers of rebels in Wexford crushed with great ferocity when local loyalists were executed on Wexford bridge. The fortunes of the seaport declined in the 20th century because of the shifting harbor sands, and the port now mainly services mussel dredgers. The opening scenes of Steven Spielberg's 1998 movie *Saving Private Ryan* were filmed on nearby Curracloe Beach. The town hosts an internationally recognized opera festival every fall. Wexford's other claim to fame is that the vast skeleton of the blue whale on display at London's Natural History Museum was found in the bay here.

Above left: Boats are moored along Wexford's waterfront in the natural harbor that is created by the estuary at the Slaney rivermouth.

Above right: Wexford was founded by Vikings who called it 'inlet of the mudflats' or Waes Fjord, from which its name evolved.

Right: In Wexford Bullring, a 1905 memorial (by Oliver Sheppard) depicts a lone bronze pikeman and remembers the failed 1798 rebellion of the United Irishmen. These bronze figures by Eamon O'Doherty located at Larkins Cross, County Wexford, were completed in 1997 and pay further tribute to their bravery.

Above: The stately house of Westport has always been the home of the Browne family line (descendants of the legendary 16th-century pirate queen Granuaile of Connaught) with the present occupant being the tenth Marquis of Sligo. In 1732 the east façade was designed to serve as part of a classical mansion, laid out around the earlier fortified house. Woodlands were planted and waterfalls fashioned across the river.

Right: Stone bridges cross the River Carrowbeg in Westport, County Mayo. Much of the present — and very elegant — Georgian town was commissioned by Lord Sligo of Westport House as a place of residence for his tenants and workers. The town lies in the shadow of Croagh Patrick where the saint was said to have spent the Lent season in AD 441 on the mountaintop, praying and fasting.

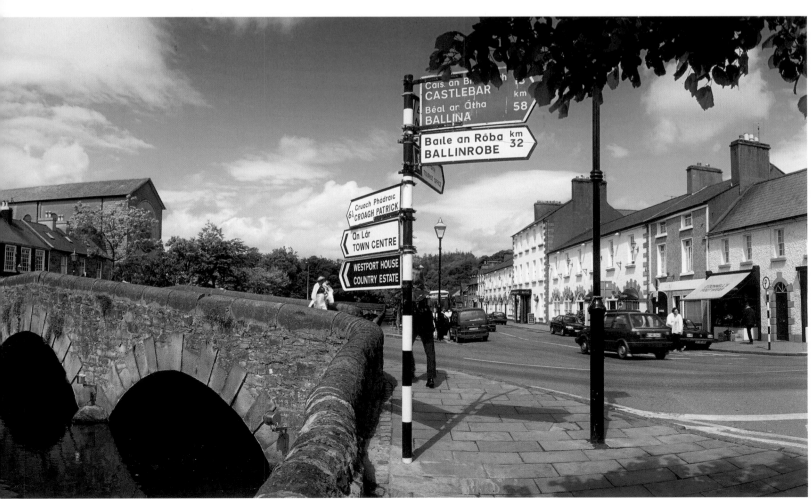

Youghal

Set at the mouth of the picturesque River Blackwater, Youghal in County Cork is an excellent example of a Norman walled port. Visitors can follow in the wake of earlier residents Sir Walter Raleigh, who was mayor in 1588, Edmund Spenser, who wrote some of *The Faerie Queene* here, and Sir Richard Boyle, sheriff from 1625–26, to explore a fascinating town, its streets lined with colorful Victorian shopfronts. There are many medieval dwellings, the 15th-century tower house of Tyntes Castle and 17th-century almshouses. A sturdy, arched 18th-century Clock Gate straddles the main street where the Red House, a 1710 Dutch-style mansion built for the Uniake family is also found.

Long ago, Youghal was occupied by Danes and then Normans. It received a charter from King John and was part of the lands granted to Sir Walter Raleigh whose home, Myrtle Grove, still stands. The stories tell how it was here that Raleigh planted the first potatoes in Europe but some historians might dispute this! The town was used to replicate New Bedford, Massachusetts, in John Huston's 1956 movie *Moby Dick*.

Above: The old arch and clock tower in Youghal (top) spans a narrow street. The town was used during the filming of the John Huston version of Moby Dick, *starring Gregory Peck. Residents (above) watch the waterfront alterations that transform their port into New Bedford, Massachusetts, a US whaling center in the 1850s.*

Opposite: During the 16th century, Youghal was the second most important British trading port. Famous Elizabethans associated with the town include the great poet Edmund Spenser as well as writer, courtier, and explorer Sir Walter Raleigh (portrayed here) who lived in Youghal and was its mayor in 1588 and 1589.

CHAPTER 4

THE IRISH WAY OF LIFE

From downing a pint of Guinness in a busy pub to being enthralled by tales of leprechauns and banshees ... from playing the traditional fiddle or the bagpipes to listening to world-class rock bands ... from watching small fishing boats set sail to gazing at ships plowing through the ocean toward America ... from enjoying wonderful plays, stories, and poetry to the excitement of a hurling match or betting at the races ... the way of life in Ireland is never dull. It is bursting with vigor and enthusiasm, imagination, and an unquenchable Irish spirit.

Above: *Dublin's lively Temple Bar district is full of places to eat and drink. It is a great place to meet up with friends.*

Left: *With fly-fishing popular on rivers and lakes and sea angling on the coast, many a plump salmon or trout is served for supper.*

Through the centuries, the way of life in Ireland has been influenced by the waves of invaders who have sailed to the island's shores and sought to rule over her people, building homes, forts, and castles, governing sometimes benignly and sometimes cruelly, dominating but never really subjugating the Irish people and their unquenchable spirit. Over the years, Vikings, Normans, and the English have come and gone; some of these visitors married Irish colleens and their children absorbed the influence of both their Irish forebears and those of the newer arrivals.

Above: A Viking confronts King Brian Ború, who ruled from the early 11th century until 1014. He subjugated Munster, then extended his control over southern Ireland until by 1002 he was High King. Relations with the Norse rulers worsened as his power increased.

Right: The romantic ruins of medieval Dunluce Castle date back to the 13th century and now seem to grow out of the sea-bound promontory. It was probably built or restructured by Richard de Burgh or one of his followers during Anglo-Norman times.

Historic backdrop

Unlike so much of the rest of Europe, the Romans never invaded this land, so Ireland's heroic high kings ruled on beyond the time when the early history of Ireland was shrouded in legend, with warring gods and giants peopling many a long-told tale. Celts raised their standing dolmens and stone circles at least 2000 years BC while druids upheld pagan rituals until Christian missionaries, like Saint Patrick and Saint Brigid, arrived and converted the Irish. As a result, Christian monasteries, abbeys, cathedrals, and then schools and colleges became a significant feature of Ireland's landscape. Many mighty fortifications, beautiful places of worship, and fine houses were part of the heritage left by these successive invaders as the long centuries passed.

Irish chiefs held sway until their submission to the Anglo-Norman rule of Henry II in 1169. At the time of the Reformation Henry VIII's creation of the new Church of England in 1532 created a furore in Ireland as the Catholic population resisted the imposition of the new Protestant faith. Catholic opposition to English rule broke out into armed rebellion during the English Civil War, but this was brutally put down by Oliver Cromwell's Irish campaign in 1649–50. In 1690 supporters of the deposed Catholic King James II were defeated at the Battle of the Boyne by William III's army. This gave the English victory but never full control — fierce opposition to English rule continued in the ensuing centuries.

Above: At the Battle of the Boyne on 1 July 1690, King William of Orange defeated the supporters of exiled James II. It is often viewed as a vital turning point in the struggle between Protestant and Catholic interests in Ireland but, in fact, both armies included adherents to both faiths. However, it did put an end to James's attempt to regain the thrones of England and Scotland.

Opposite: Here Saint Patrick is depicted with his foot upon a snake, referring to his legendary expulsion from Irish soil of every serpent — the embodiment of evil and pagan religions. One tale tells how Saint Patrick made a box and invited the wily snake to enter. The serpent insisted it was too small but, finally, to prove his point, slithered inward. The saint slammed the lid and tossed the box and its hissing contents into the sea.

Above: During the Great Famine in the 1840s when the potato crop failed, many poor tenants were evicted from their smallholdings as the inevitable penury left them unable to pay the rent. Here, adding to the cruelty, the thatched roof is being removed to prevent reoccupation. Entire families were left starving, homeless, and exposed to cholera. In July 1848, the number of famine victims seeking relief peaked at almost 840,000.

DEPARTURE OF THE "NIMROD" AND "ATHLONE" STEAMERS, WITH EMIGRANTS ON BOARD, FOR LIVERPOOL.

Above: 1851 — steamships Nimrod and Athlone depart from Cork, taking emigrants to Liverpool and thence to America. The potato famine was a major human catastrophe and, throughout the 19th century, many Irish sought new lives elsewhere. But terrible conditions on board ship meant that typhus, easily spread by body lice in such cramped conditions, would kill hundreds before they even glimpsed the New World across the ocean.

The Great Famine

All this while, ordinary folk tilled the soil, growing produce and caring for their farm animals until the potato blight and Great Famine of 1845-51 wreaked havoc to the staple crop. This was a black period in Irish history with so many slow deaths (some 2 million people are thought to have died), mass emigration to escape the privations, and the scattering of families and countless Irish abroad. Many of the survivors left behind faced ruin as agricultural prices plummeted, farmers fell into arrears, and workers were evicted from the land.

Ultimately the campaign for Home Rule grew ever stronger until the Easter Rising in 1916 when members of the Irish Volunteers and Irish Citizen Army took up arms against British rule. The rebellion was brutally quashed with its 16 leaders court-martialed and peremptorily shot — resulting in their status as martyrs and all adding strength to the Irish cause. In 1920, a political solution was reached and Ireland was divided, with the South becoming fully independent by 1937. Nonetheless, unrest and terror persisted because predominantly Protestant Northern Ireland remained part of the United Kingdom.

The period from 1969 to the 1990s was marked by violence and terrorism, but at last, in 1998, the Good Friday Agreement was signed and the inauguration of the Northern Ireland Assembly paved the way for peace between the battling communities. A member of the European Economic Community since 1973, The Republic of Ireland has now grown into a prosperous modern nation with the Euro adopted as its currency in 2002. Today the Republic's turbulent but magnificent history and its fine heritage together form the foundation for a forward-looking, thriving nation.

Left: Daniel O'Connell, the 'Liberator,' campaigned to repeal laws penalizing Irish Roman Catholics, seeking their right to sit at the Westminster Parliament. In 1830, he became the first Catholic in modern history to sit in the House of Commons. In 1840, he founded the Repeal Association, aiming to abolish the Union with Britain and establish an Irish parliament.

Below: The 1916 Easter Rising in Dublin left Sackville Street (now called O'Connell Street) in a state of utter devastation. The Rising was suppressed after six days of fighting, and its leaders were vilified and court-martialed. Many were executed and as a result were honored as martyrs. In due course this invigorated the surge toward Irish independence.

Irish writers

Ireland has an incredible Gaelic heritage with the oldest vernacular literature in Europe. Much of the Celtic folklore was written down in monastic times but the rich flow of Gaelic literature vanished along with the Irish aristocracy in the 17th century when the flight of Hugh O'Neill and Hugh O'Donnell into exile in 1607 was seen as the passing of the old Gaelic order in the face of overwhelming English authority. Today, the places of residence of Irish authors are marked with plaques while many major figures and their works are highlighted in the Literary Parade, a monument to Irish writers in Dublin's St Patrick's Park. There is even more to be discovered in the Dublin Writers Museum, which houses a history and celebration of literary Dublin. With so many famous Irish authors, writing in English and in Gaelic, only a smattering of the most illustrious and their many works can be mentioned here.

Dramatist, novelist, and Nobel Prize winner, Samuel Beckett best known for his play *Waiting for Godot*, was born in Dublin; he studied and lectured at Trinity College, where he graduated, as did … Oliver Goldsmith (who wrote *The Vicar of Wakefield* and *She Stoops to Conquer*), Jonathan Swift (Dean of Dublin's St Patrick's Cathedral and author of *Gulliver's Travels*), Bram Stoker, most remembered as the author of *Dracula*, and the famous wit Oscar Wilde, whose many works include *The Importance of Being Earnest*, *Lady Windermere's Fan*, and *The Picture of Dorian Gray*.

Dublin-born Richard Brinsley Sheridan's elopement to France with a young girl resulted in his being challenged to a duel and seriously wounded, a suitably romantic interlude for an author famous for his popular comedies *The Rivals* and *The School for Scandal*. Nobel Prize winner George Bernard Shaw was born in Dublin and worked in an office there: his most famous plays include *Saint Joan* and *Arms and the Man*. More recent writers include Sean O'Casey (who wrote stirring plays like *Shadow of a Gunman*) and James Joyce, probably best known for his Dublin novel *Ulysses*. The many other Irish names of note include Brendan Behan, Edna O'Brien, Roddy Doyle, George Farquhar, Brian Friel, Seamus Heaney, and John Millington Synge.

Over the last century or so, many Irish playwrights and actors have honed their skills at Dublin's renowned Abbey

Theater: it opened in 1904 — with playwright and author Lady Augusta Gregory, and poet and dramatist William Butler Yeats among its founders. Thoor Ballylee Castle in County Galway was once the home of W.B. Yeats and the Tower here is now a fitting monument to the author. The 16th-century medieval tower house, originally built by the de Burgo (or Burke) family, has four one-room floors linked by a spiral stone stairway. Yeats made this his summer home for 12 years and was inspired to write *The Winding Stair* and *The Tower Poems* here. Today it is a Yeats museum, with some first editions.

Opposite: A plaque marks the birthplace of James Joyce.

Above left: Trinity College Library houses some four million volumes which have been collected since the late 16th century.

Top: Oscar Wilde, the son of a renowned surgeon and a lady poet, wrote many superbly witty plays and was a great celebrity.

Above: Oliver Goldsmith, the renowned Anglo-Irish author and poet, once planned to emigrate to America but he missed the ferry!

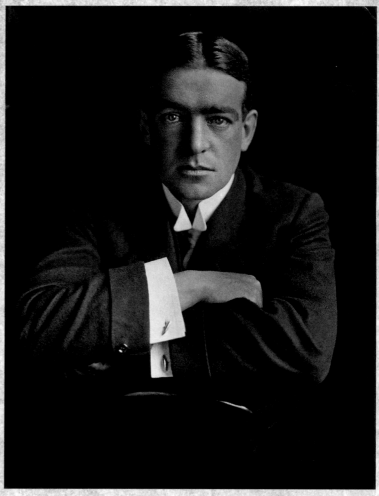

Other famous Irish people

Historians relate that Saint Brendan the Navigator was born around 484 in County Kerry and founded monasteries, including Clonfert (County Galway) where he was buried in 577 at the then-remarkable age of 93. There are fascinating claims that this brave missionary made a legendary seven-year voyage, sailing to France — and then America — in a boat not unlike the currachs made in County Kerry today. In 1976, navigation scholar and explorer Tim Severin sailed from Brandon Creek on the Dingle peninsula in a currach constructed to match the details recorded by Brendan. He saw whales, possibly the great 'sea-monsters' the monk had described and then overwintered in Iceland where volcanoes might well have been erupting when Brendan and his companions reported being pelted with 'flaming, foul smelling rocks.' As the voyage progressed, he passed icebergs (the legend described 'towering crystals') and ultimately crossed the Atlantic to land at Newfoundland, thus proving such a voyage feasible.

Antarctic explorer, Ernest Shackleton, was born in Kilkea, County Kildare in 1874. A member of Scott's *Discovery* Expedition in 1901–02, he returned to Antarctica in 1907, traveling to within 97 miles (156km) of the South Pole and then again in 1914, this time in the ill-fated *Endurance* that was trapped when frozen into crushing ice. This episode triggered Shackleton's renowned epic escape in an open boat when he voyaged across 800 miles (1300km) of treacherous ocean to land on South Georgia and then climbed high mountains to reach a whaling station and organize the rescue of his crew who were stranded on Elephant Island. Shackleton died in 1922 in South Georgia at the age of 47, on his fourth Antarctic expedition. The Athy Heritage Center (Kildare) is the only museum in Ireland that honors him.

Above left: Tim Severin; explorer, film-maker, writer, and lecturer who set out to prove that Brendan the Navigator could have reached the Americas in the 6th century.

Above right: Ernest H. Shackleton (1874-1922) went on several expeditions to Antarctica and is famous for his bravery and brilliant leadership skills. He was born in Kilkea, County Kildare.

Opposite: Some of the Guinness family fortune contributed to the restoration of 12th-century St Patrick's Cathedral in Dublin, which had been raised on the site where Saint Patrick is said to have baptized Christian converts.

Beer and books

Sir Arthur Guinness was born in Celbridge (County Kildare) in 1725; his father was land steward to the Archbishop of Cashel and brewed beer for workers on the estate. In due course, Arthur Guinness established the now-famous brewery in Dublin, making dark porter beer from malted barley. At that time, beer was almost unknown in rural Ireland where whiskey, gin, and poteen were favored tipples. In time, St James's Gate became the largest porter and stout brewery in the world on a site for which Arthur Guinness had astutely procured — in what is now a most sought-after area — a £45 per annum lease for 9000 years! Guinness spent his last years at Beaumont, his country home in Drumcondra, now a Dublin suburb, and died in 1803. By 1838, his Dublin brewery was Ireland's largest; it continued to grow and was soon exporting worldwide. In due course, the Guinness family wealth contributed to the restoration of St Patrick's Cathedral. The company also launched the renowned *Guinness Book of Records* in 1951 after Sir Hugh Beaver (then brewery managing director) was involved in a dispute when on a shooting party as to which was the swifter gamebird — grouse or golden plover. His inability to find an answer in the reference books available led him to commission a book that would supply answers to this, and thousands of other similar questions.

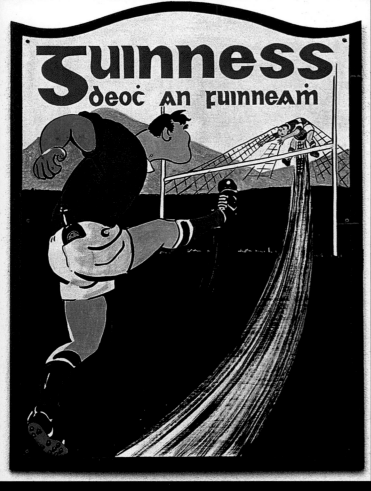

These pages: Guinness uses the Brian Ború harp as its trademark. From the 1930s, brilliant advertising often featuring a toucan appeared on pub signs, posters, television, and beer mats. Examples are now very collectable.

Opposite below: A 1953 scene; a worker pushes a barrow of malt samples. The Guinness complex at St James's Gate, Dublin, is a vast 62-acre (25-hectare) site but the premises were secured in 1759 by Arthur Guinness for a minimal rent on a 9000-year lease. The Guinness Storehouse visitor center, on the site of the original brewery, is Ireland's prime international visitor attraction, visited by millions since it opened in 2000. Guinness is still brewed here at the largest stout brewery in the world.

Above: Bob Geldof, the renowned musician and former lead singer with The Boomtown Rats, is known as a remarkable humanitarian, political activist, and fund-raiser who initiated the Band Aid and Live Aid projects. Born in 1951 in Dún Laoghaire, County Dublin, he was given the Freedom of the City of Dublin in 2006 in recognition of his continuing campaigning against injustice, debt, famine, starvation, disease, AIDS, and for fathers' rights.

Top: Bono, lead singer of the Irish rock band U2, was born and raised in Dublin. In 2000, the four members of U2 were given the Freedom of the City of Dublin and Bono is here depicted with guitarist David Howell Evans (known as The Edge) holding lambs because, together with this honor, comes the traditional right to graze sheep in St Stephen's Green in the center of the city.

The Irish impact

Many famous film stars, musicians, and entertainers hail from the island of Ireland. These include Bono and U2, Boyzone, Kenneth Branagh, Wilfred Brambell, Pierce Brosnan (of James Bond fame), Gabriel Byrne, Sinéad O'Connor, James Galway, Bob Geldof and The Boomtown Rats, Richard Harris, Daniel Day-Lewis, Spike Milligan, Van Morrison, Liam Neeson, the Nolans, Maureen O'Hara, Maureen O'Sullivan (Ireland's first film star), Peter O'Toole, Thin Lizzy, and Westlife.

Across the Atlantic, American actors and directors James Cagney, George Clooney, Bing Crosby, Tom Cruise, Walt Disney, John Ford, Judy Garland, and Grace Kelly are among the many who have claimed Irish heritage. A total of 35,975,855 Americans (around 12 percent of the total population) reported Irish ancestry in the 2006 American Community Survey while worldwide it is said that some 70 million people can claim Irish descent.

Presidents with Irish blood

At least 23 US presidents have claimed to have Irish blood — including Chester Arthur, George W. Bush, Ulysses S. Grant (his family's restored cottage at Ballygawley still has mud floors), Andrew Jackson whose parents emigrated in 1765 from a thatched cottage in Carrickfergus, James K. Polk, and Ronald Reagan. The farm from which the grandfather of Woodrow Wilson emigrated in 1807 is near Strabane — and is still occupied by the Wilson family. President John F. Kennedy was a practicing Catholic with clear Irish lineage: his maternal great-grandparents were driven out from County Limerick by the devastating potato famine while his paternal great-grandfather left County Wexford at much the same time to sail to Boston from New Ross. President Kennedy visited Ireland in June 1963 and remarked 'This is not the land of my birth but it is the land for which I hold the greatest affection.'

Opposite: Several US presidents have claimed to have Irish blood including the 35th President, John F. Kennedy, who was the great-grandson of Irish immigrants and the only Irish-Catholic American President of the United States. He first visited his ancestral home in 1947 but here he is seen at a family reunion on a visit to Dunganstown in June 1963, just a few months before his tragic assassination on November 22 in Dallas, Texas.

Above left: Actor George Clooney plans to visit Cork and tour around on a Harley motorbike, seeking his 'Cooney' cousins. When Irish people emigrated to America many names were misspelt on arrival and George's relatives gained an 'l' as well as a new nation.

Above right: Ronald Reagan claimed Irish heritage. Pioneers Buffalo Bill Cody, Daniel Boone, and Davy Crockett also had Irish ancestry, as did Henry Ford of the motor-car company.

Top right: The grandfather of Grace Kelly (film star and Princess of Monaco) left Ireland in 1867. She loved collecting Irish literature and music, a collection ultimately gathered in Monaco's Princess Grace Irish Library. It contains Irish music sheets and 8000 books, with works by James Joyce, Samuel Beckett, Oscar Wilde, George Bernard Shaw, and W.B. Yeats.

Influence in America

Many Americans of Irish descent have contributed hugely to their newly adopted homelands. For example, John Dunlap, first apprenticed at Gray's Printing Press in Strabane (County Tyrone), went on to found America's first daily newspaper, the *Pennsylvania Packet* and then, moreover, to print one of the most famous documents in the world — the Declaration of Independence.

The Ulster-American Folk Park (near Omagh, County Tyrone) developed around the cottage where Thomas Mellon was born in 1813. His family emigrated to Pennsylvania when Thomas was five and he grew up to become a judge, founder of Mellon Bank, and patriarch of an immensely wealthy family. His son, Andrew, was secretary to the US Treasury in the 1920s, ambassador to London, Pittsburgh's chief architect, and possibly the richest man in the world at that time. Mellon money helped to fund the construction of the Waldorf Astoria, the Panama Canal's locks and gates, and San Francisco's Golden Gate Bridge.

Above and far left: The family of Thomas Mellon emigrated to Pennsylvania in 1818. He became a millionaire and the family fortune helped to fund the famous New York hotel, the Waldorf Astoria, as well as San Francisco's landmark, the Golden Gate Bridge.

Left: The Declaration of Independence was printed by one John Dunlap, originally apprenticed at Gray's Printing Press in Strabane (County Tyrone).

The wealthy lifestyle

Most of those who emigrated from Ireland during the famine period were leaving humble homes to seek a new and better life. Meanwhile, the wealthier folk usually stayed put and their fine ancestral homes are here to prove it!

Ireland's many magnificent houses include Powerscourt House and Gardens near Enniskerry, in the foothills of the Wicklow Mountains. This elegant Palladian house erected in the 18th century on the site of an earlier castle, and reached by a mile-long avenue flanked by some 2000 beech trees, has a lovely restored double-height Georgian ballroom. Outside, a fine terrace and statues lead to formal, Japanese, Italianate, and walled gardens with 200 varieties of trees and shrubs, ornamental lakes, and secret shady hollows. Nearby is Powerscourt waterfall, its 398ft (121m) drop making it Ireland's highest.

Built between 1741 and 1753, Russborough House is set in Blessington, near the borders of counties Kildare and Wicklow. This is also in Palladian style with colonnades, wide wings, and an elegant flight of steps. There are heraldic lions and baroque urns, while the lavish interior has stucco ceilings, great mantelpieces, inlaid floors, and lavish mahogany doors and staircases. The superb collection of paintings (including works by Gainsborough, Rubens, and Goya) has unfortunately attracted four robberies, with two paintings being stolen twice … but ultimately recovered.

Palatial homes

Splendid Castletown House (built between 1722 and 1729) is the largest and possibly grandest Palladian country house in Ireland, built for William Conolly, then Speaker of the Irish House of Commons. He had risen from humble origins to

make a fortune out of land transactions and become the wealthiest man in Ireland. The Conolly family continued to live here until 1965 when the estate was sold to a property developer. It was purchased in 1967 by Desmond Guinness, founder of the Irish Georgian Society, in an attempt to rescue it from vandalism. It is now managed by the Office of Public Works. The façade, by Alessandro Galilei, emulates a 16th-century Italian city palace with curving Palladian colonnades and substantial wings; within are many superb richly decorated rooms, a 80ft (24m) Pompeian-style Long Gallery plus a huge Portland stone cantilevered staircase.

Reached by a hundred steps, Bantry House is a stately home overlooking Bantry Bay that was developed from an 18th-century Queen Anne mansion; today, three centuries later, the wings house bed and breakfast accommodation while

the central core remains a veritable treasure house containing wonderful paintings, prints, china, chandeliers, and elegant furnishings. Many were collected by the second Earl of Bantry during his European travels and the tapestries include one believed to have been owned by Marie Antoinette. The first Earl, Richard White, gained his title by showing his loyalty to Britain and informing British forces of the proposed invasion of Wolfe Tone and the United Irishmen in 1796. The carriage house and stable block here house a French Armada Center with lots of information about the abortive attempt by the French fleet to land 14,000 troops in Bantry Bay. Subtropical plants and shrubs thrive in 45 acres (18 hectares) of grounds which feature marble statues, the stepped gardens and parterres that comprise the 'Staircase to the Sky,' a gorgeous Italian garden, and Ireland's largest wisteria circle.

Above: Russborough House is in fine Palladian style and was designed by the renowned architect Richard Cassels.

Top: Castletown House is a simply magnificent building which made the most of Irish craftsmen and materials when it was built in the 1720s for William Conolly, Speaker of the Irish House of Commons.

Opposite: Powerscourt House in County Wicklow is set in 47 acres (19 hectares) of glorious gardens established by the third Viscount.

Myths, legends, and fairies

Among the mists and hills of Ireland, many myths and legends were forged, several with ancient Celtic origins and some relating to the high kings and to Christian saints that were portrayed in legend as miracle-workers with the power to banish monsters, cure illnesses, and feed the hungry. Some wells are considered holy and there are those whose waters are said to effect cures. Many are dedicated to particular saints and are an important part of their feast-day celebrations. The most celebrated Irish saints are patron saint Patrick, monk, priest, and missionary Columba (born in County Donegal) and Brigid, who protected farms and livestock.

Legendary giants and heroes

Legends of giants were spawned by the gigantic natural wonders of the Irish landscape as well as from the ancient remains and fortifications that these mighty men were believed to have built. One of the most famous mythical hunter-warriors was Fionn Mac Cumhaill (anglicized as Finn McCool) from whom the 19th-century nationalist Fenian movement took its name. The son of Cumhall and Muirne (a

druid's daughter) he was brought up in secret in a forest, and served several local kings and a druid — until one day he inadvertently swallowed a piece of skin from the salmon of knowledge, thereby gaining special powers and great wisdom.

Finn McCool rescued the men of Tara from the fairy Aillen and married Sadbh who was ultimately turned into a deer — but not before she had given birth to Oisin, their fine son. Oisin grew up to be a wise poet and one of the greatest of the Fianna, warrior bands who lived in the forests but could be called upon by kings in times of war. In legend, Finn McCool triumphed over many giants and magicians and is supposed to have built the Giant's Causeway (see page 62). Popular legends claim that the giant still sleeps in a cave below Dublin, ready to awake and defend Ireland when need be.

Another mythological hero is Cúchulainn who appears in the Ulster Cycle, a body of medieval heroic legends. He killed Culann's fierce guard-dog in self-defense when only a child and then assumed its role until a replacement could be reared. When aged just 17, Cúchulainn defended Ulster single-handedly against the armies of Queen Medb (or Maeve) of Connacht. He was renowned for his terrifying battle fury when he swelled up and turned different colors: the heat of his body melted snow all around as he glowed red; if he bathed, the water hissed and turned to steam.

Other stories tell how champion and hero Lugh, a Celtic god of blacksmiths and artisans, had to slay his grandfather who was a tyrant with an evil eye that destroyed all upon whom he gazed. Even Julius Caesar was aware of Lugh's importance to the Celtic people and his battlefield renown. When Lugh arrived at Tara, the hall of the high kings of Ireland, the guard refused him entry as only one individual with any particular skill was allowed inside and there was already someone within for each of Lugh's attributes. With classic Irish wit, Lugh finally gained entry upon suggesting that he was surely the only one able to master them *all*.

Left: Saint Columba blessing apples; this Gaelic missionary monk (one of the Twelve Apostles of Erin) was a great-great-grandson of Niall of the Nine Hostages, a 5th-century Irish High King. He studied at Clonard Abbey but eventually settled on the Scottish island of Iona, the center of his mission to convert the Picts.

Opposite: Legends tell how the great Finn McCool could split rock into columns with an ax that had an elephant-sized blade. He reputedly built the Giant's Causeway so that he could cross the sea to fight his Scottish adversary, Benandonner.

The little people

As well as the heroes and great giants that once stalked the land and reputedly strode across the sea to Scotland, Irish legends are peopled by the 'little folk.' The people of the aos sí (pronounced ess she) developed from early Celtic beliefs that the dead live on in splendid style within fairy burial mounds. Ancient earthwork structures dot the landscape here and many stories are told of humans being escorted to these hidden palaces at night to attend wondrous banquets. In a similar way, fairies were believed to live under mounds of earth called 'raths' and many fairyfolk are associated with the ancient burial places, stone circles, and earthworks found in Ireland. Some are benevolent but a good number are malevolent — or a mix of both. Red is often seen as the color of magic and the caps of fairies are generally scarlet. They adore music, especially the Celtic harp or violin, and may befriend the finest players.

Many Celtic folk believe that the aos sí are an ancient tall race that rule the fairy kingdom and, once, ruled all of Ireland too. Sometimes the fairies take a handsome healthy human child to their fairy palaces, leaving a sickly deformed youngster in its place — a changeling, known as *iarlais* in Ireland. This skinny howling creature has dark penetrating eyes, yellow skin, and often a lame, clawed hand or crooked back. It is generally malicious, voraciously hungry, but very wise. In the old days, admiring a beautiful new baby was said to put it in danger of being snatched, while left-handed people might be suspected of being changelings. While they drain good fortune from their host families, changelings are welcomed in pubs as brilliant fiddle and pipe players.

Left: From an 1870 book, this illustration by Richard Doyle (a notable Victorian illustrator) depicts tiny fairy folk.

Background: 'An Elfin Dance by Night' by Richard Doyle. An atmospheric illustration of the kind of magical world that forms part of the folklore of the Emerald Isle.

Leprechauns and banshees

There are many types of fairy or elf in the folklore of the Emerald Isle. The most renowned is the leprechaun, generally perceived as a small mischievous bearded old man in a tall hat, green or red tunic, and with buckled shoes. Usually he has a shoemaker's or a cobbler's skills, and leads a solitary life in lonely country places. He will have buried a crock of gold somewhere — often at the end of a rainbow — but is a cunning fellow and will not reveal the secret of its location. Once caught, a leprechaun cannot escape while being watched but never seems to be successfully tricked into disclosing the gold's whereabouts before diverting his captor's attention and then rushing away to freedom. The leprechaun is often associated with another fairy figure — the surly clurichaun who enjoys boozing sprees and will look after your drinks cellar as long as you do not object to his taking rides on your sheep, geese, goats, and dogs! If you mistreat them, they will ruin your cellar of wine. A *far darrig* (or red man) is another type of fairy: he wears a red coat and cap but is jeering and mischievous, enjoying playing rather gruesome practical jokes on unsuspecting victims.

Banshees are female spirits, said to wail outside a house where death is imminent, particularly attending the five major Irish families (the O'Neills, O'Briens, O'Connors, O'Gradys, and Kavanaghs) and the courts of Irish kings. A banshee's three main guises — a young woman, a stately matron, or raddled old hag — represent the triple aspects (Badhbh, Macha, and Mor-Rioghain) of the Celtic goddess of war and death. She generally gives vent to her mourning wail dressed in a gray, hooded cloak, a corpse's winding sheet, or in washerwoman's garb but she may also appear as a hooded crow, stoat, hare, or weasel.

Other fairy folk

The dullahan is a wild and black-robed headless horseman, who may appear at midnight at Irish festivals or be seen riding a black steed that snorts sparks and flames. The dullahan uses the backbone of a human corpse as a whip. His head (that looks like stale dough or moldy cheese and has an idiotic grin) is carried on the saddle or held high in his right hand, glowing to light his way. Wherever the dullahan stops, someone dies. Anyone trying to spy on him may be blinded in one eye or doused in a basin of blood, which is an omen of death. He usually rides his ghostly steed in the remoter parts of Counties Sligo and Down, while in County Tyrone, he drives a black coach pulled by six black horses, setting fire to the bushes as he flies by. Even locked gates swing open to let him pass. The only substance to induce fear into a dullahan is gold.

The fearsome pooka is a shape-changer. It may appear as a gleaming horse with a long wild mane and sulfurous yellow eyes, charging through the fields at night, trampling crops and scattering livestock so that hens refuse to lay and cows to give milk. Another guise is a deformed goblin who demands a share of the harvest — a 'pooka's share' was often left by reapers. In County Laois he may assume the role of a great hairy bogeyman; in Waterford and Wexford he is a massive eagle; and in Roscommon, a black goat with twisted horns. He may hurl night travelers into muddy ditches or bogholes or call out the names of those he wants to take on a midnight dash, vandalizing the property of those who refuse this dubious pleasure.

A grogoch is a half-human, half-fairy male figure whose forebears are believed to have come from Kintyre in Scotland to north Antrim, Rathlin Island, and parts of Donegal. These are small ancient creatures, generally naked but covered in rough reddish hair or fur, as well as matted twigs and dirt. They can make themselves invisible, only allowing trusted people to see them. They usually live in a cave or hollow or under large leaning stones. Sometimes they help with planting, harvesting, and household chores in exchange for a jug of cream and will bustle about the kitchen. They are afraid only of men of the Church.

Right: Water spirits include the Bean-Fionn (or Jenny Greentooth) who lives beneath lakes and streams and who reaches out to drag any children playing nearby under the water.

Water spirits

The merrow is a water spirit, rather like a mermaid, who may warn fishermen of gales. Male merrows or mermen have red noses, green teeth and hair, pig-like eyes, and webbed scales between their fingers. The female merrow, however, may be beautiful — and promiscuous — and can also assume the shape of a seal. While on land merrows may become small hornless cows. Merrows wear a red cap called a *cohullen druith*, often covered with feathers; they cannot return to the sea if this cap is stolen or hidden so a fisherman may secrete this cap and persuade a merrow to marry him and help him locate gold plundered from shipwrecks. However, if she can retrieve her cap, she will escape back to the sea at the earliest opportunity, abandoning both husband and children. Many old Irish families rather poetically claim merrow descent.

Saint Patrick's Day celebrations

Of all the Irish celebrations, undoubtedly the merriment that takes place on Saint Patrick's Day (March 17, unless this falls inappropriately in Holy Week) is the most well known. Saint Patrick was born in Wales in about AD 385 but, when 16, was sold into slavery by a group of Irish raiders. After six years, he escaped and studied in a monastery in Gaul for a dozen years during which time he became aware that his vocation was to convert nonbelievers to Christianity. He landed in Wicklow in 432 and began his mission in Ireland. Eventually he was appointed second bishop to Ireland and set about winning converts — much to the chagrin of the Celtic druids. Patrick was arrested and escaped several times as he traveled throughout Ireland, establishing monasteries, schools and churches in a 30-year mission. He died on March 17 in 461.

Because Saint Patrick used the three-leafed shamrock in his sermons to explain the nature of the Holy Trinity, this became a symbol for his feast day and now shamrocks are blazoned everywhere. The traditional Saint Patrick's Day meal was Irish bacon and cabbage to accompany what was essentially a religious festival. Now, however, Saint Patrick's Day has mutated into the most famous Irish grand party with processions, a good deal of drinking and the consumption of food that may even be dyed green! This is Ireland's national holiday but the celebrations are shared all around the globe, wherever Irish people live.

In fact the first Saint Patrick's Day parade took place in the United States when Irish soldiers serving in the English military, wanting to reconnect with their Irish roots, marched through New York City on March 17 1762. Now Dublin city rocks to five days of music, street theater, carnivals, dancing, treasure hunts, night spectacles, and fireworks — culminating in the famous Saint Patrick's Day Parade that up to 500,000 people may attend.

Opposite above left: The Saint Patrick's Day parade marches up Fifth Avenue in New York as jubilant spectators cheer them on.

Opposite above right: A boy with his face painted in the Irish national colors wraps an Irish flag around his shoulders.

Opposite: Uillean bagpipers march along Dublin's Patrick Street as the parade weaves through the city center. Over five days, some 4000 performers and a million or so people celebrate with music, street theater, and dance in the carnival atmosphere of Ireland's biggest annual party.

Above: Flag-carrying firefighters march in the Saint Patrick's Day parade in New York (top), when there is an extravaganza of celebration. In Chicago (above) the river is dyed bright green in honor of the Emerald Isle and its patron saint's commemorative day.

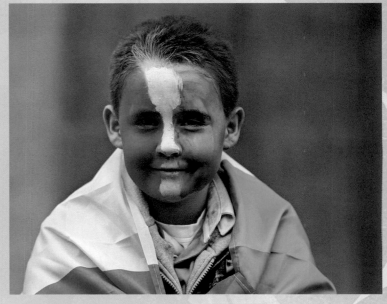

"St. Patrick's Day in the Morning."

The Wearing of the Green.

St. Patrick's Day Fond Memories

ERIN GO BRACH

PIPE OF PEACE

THE TOP O' THE MORNIN' TO YOU.

A Victorian tradition

There are many familiar Irish elements that contribute to the annual Saint Patrick's Day celebrations, such as the color green, the shamrock, and leprechauns with their tall hats and pipes. The traditions have been passed from generation to generation as these Victorian greeting cards depict.

Moving clockwise from top left they show dancers jigging to 'St Patrick's Day in the Morning'; a young girl in her emerald finery; a boy and girl sitting upright in high-backed chairs in 'St Patrick's Day — Fond memories'; gentlemen smoking and shaking hands in 'The Top o' the Mornin' to you'; and a pot of shamrocks in 'The Wearing of the Green.' Meanwhile, the Saint Patrick's Day greeting cards shown on the right depict Blarney Castle and Ross Castle respectively.

The wearing of the green also marks the first green of spring. On this special Irish Holiday, March 17, all things Irish are celebrated. As one traditional song says:

St Patrick, the holy and tutular man
His beard down his bosom like Aaron's ran:
Some from Scotland, some from Wales, will declare
that he came,
But I care not from whence now he's risen to fame;
The pride of the world and his enemies scorning
I will drink to St Patrick, today in the morning!
He's a desperate big, little Erin go brah;
He will pardon our follies and promise us joy,
By the mass, by the Pope, by St Patrick so long
As I live, I will give him a beautiful song!
No saint is so good, Ireland's country adorning:
Then hail to St Patrick, today, in the morning.

Enjoying Irish sport

As part of the Gaelic revival, the Gaelic Athletic Association (GAA) was founded in 1884 to promote native Irish sports, such as hurling, Gaelic football, and handball. The season draws to a close with the All-Ireland Hurling and Football Finals in Dublin that attract vast enthusiastic crowds.

Hurling — played with a curved stick called a hurley — has been an Irish pastime for at least 2000 years and is the national game. Hockey developed from it in England. It was possibly the forerunner of golf too. In one version, the ball was batted back and forth over a fence, an exercise which may have served as the beginnings of tennis! During the 18th century the landed gentry organized hurling contests but as their influence diminished in the 19th century, the games often turned into rowdy affairs that women were advised to avoid. Today, played by teams of 15, this is a very fast and skillful game. Camogie, the women's version played with a shorter stick, is also very popular.

Once the GAA had been founded in 1884, the evolution of hurling into hockey was inevitable and Ireland's hockey rules were drawn up in 1892. One year later, the Irish Hockey Union was formed and the oldest hockey cup in the world, the Irish Senior Cup, was first competed for in 1894. The first international hockey game (against Wales) was played in Ireland one year later. Hurling's potentially dangerous striking and lashing at the ball was controlled in hockey by the 'rule of sticks' that forbade the hockey stick to be raised higher than the shoulder. In 1897 the first inter-provincial match was played between Munster and Leinster and by 1899 the Irish Hockey Union was forming branches throughout Ireland.

Once upon a time, handball was played against the gable-ends of houses. It is now usually played in a four-walled court. The ball used now is a hard ball called an 'alley-cracker.' The sport is similar to squash or racquetball, but, like fives, a gloved hand is used rather than a racket.

Gaelic football and soccer

Gaelic football is played by teams of 15 players: handling the ball is allowed but there is no scrum as in rugby. The All-Ireland Final takes place at Croke Park in Dublin and is now rather more orderly than some of the 18th-century gatherings when matches were often called to a halt because of public order breaches. Offending players were rounded up and imprisoned — some were even transported.

Ireland's first association football or soccer game took place in Belfast in 1878 when two Scottish teams played at the Ulster Cricket Ground. Twelve years later, the Dublin clubs, Bohemians and Shelbourne, were formed and, by 1901, the Bohemians opened their grounds at Dalymount Park — now the Republic's principal soccer ground. In 1921, the FAI (Football Association of Ireland) was founded — ultimately making soccer the only Irish field game to split in the wake of Ireland's partition. Football in Northern Ireland is administered by the Irish Football Association which was founded in 1880.

Rugby was introduced to Ireland in the mid-1800s by English students attending Dublin's Trinity College. Soon the game was being played at many schools and colleges, while rugby clubs sprang up as the enthusiasm spread. The Irish Rugby Football Union was formed in the south in 1874 and there were various enthusiastic clubs in the north too.

Above: *In 1874, the Irish Rugby Football Union was formed. In 1878, Belfast merchant John M. McAlery introduced association football or soccer to Ireland.*

Right: *Irish football fans celebrate at Dublin's Lansdowne Road stadium, which first opened for athletics in 1872. The first international soccer game took place here on Saint Patrick's Day 1900.*

Opposite: *The All-Ireland Hurling Championships (or the Guinness Hurling Championship) is the premier hurling competition played at Dublin's Croke Park. This national sport is ancient but fast, vigorous, and an exciting spectacle to watch that attracts great crowds. The ball is struck on the ground or in the air using the hurley, a wooden stick with a flat blade, traditionally made of ash.*

Left: Loyal Irish rugby fans follow their teams all around the world. This colorful young group have traveled to Paris to support their team at the Parc des Prince stadium.

Opposite: Horseracing is always an immensely popular sport in Ireland. Professional racing on the beach at Laytown takes place at a fun once-a-year event when the tide has gone out. Steps are built into the face of the sand dunes to form the grandstand while various marquees serve as weighing rooms, bars, and cafés.

Below: A rugby scrum at a World Cup match between Ireland and Argentina. Ireland also competes annually in the Six Nations Championship for European sides (Ireland, England, Scotland, Wales, France, and Italy), which they have won outright ten times.

Ireland's first international rugby match was played against England in London in 1875 with a return match taking place in Dublin in the same year. In 1883–84 England, Ireland, Scotland, and Wales played the first Triple Crown series of matches for the Home International Championship. In the early days, this highly physical game was banned on Sundays but this rule has now been relaxed.

Horse racing

Horse racing is a traditional national sport with racing over jumps and hurdles being more popular than flat racing here. The Irish passion for horses is famous and the Curragh in County Kildare, still Ireland's most famous course, was popular for stabling and racing as long ago as the 17th century. Many famous racehorses have come from Ireland — and Irish-owned or bred horses have often dominated events. Famous champions include Grand National specialist Red Rum, Derby winner Shergar (who was stolen and disappeared after ransom demands were not met), multiple Cheltenham Gold Cup winner Best Mate, and the renowned Arkle, possibly the greatest steeplechaser of all time — bred *and* trained in Ireland.

The Emerald Isle's favorable tax regime helps to encourage a thriving thoroughbred breeding industry. Celebrated equestrian events include the Irish Champion Hurdle at Leopardstown, the Irish Grand National at Fairyhouse in County Meath, Puncheston's National Hunt Racing Festival, the Irish Derby at the Curragh, and the Dublin Horse Show.

Other popular sports

Other very popular sports in Ireland today include golf. The Royal Dublin Golf Club (founded 1885) has been situated since 1889 at Clontarf on Bull Island. The Irish Open Golf Championship moves from course to course each year in the tradition of Open championships. Ireland's long coastline and many lakes encourage plenty of enthusiastic anglers and sailors (with the Cork Week regatta being a highlight) while the English introduced cricket to Ireland via the garrison towns of Kilkenny and Ballinasloe in the early 19th century. Other popular sports include motorcyle racing, boxing, athletics (the Dublin Marathon is a major event), greyhound racing, and car rallies held around the lakes of Killarney.

Left: Ireland's car-racing teams travel all around the world to compete at international events. Back at home, Mondello Park in County Kildare boasts Ireland's only permanent international race circuit that hosts an exciting program of car and motorbike racing every year.

Above: Some sports offer a scenic bonus;
here, a golfer lines up a putt at the 18-hole
Tralee Golf Club course in Ardfert, with a
ruined tower on the beach behind him,
then blue sea and mountains beyond.
Golf writer Peter Dobereiner commented:
'As a spectacle, Tralee is in a different class
... the setting is quite the most magnificent
backdrop for a golf course I have ever
encountered.'

Left: A golfer in Killarney gazes across
Lough Leane; three superb golf courses
offer firm fairways and perfect greens
beside the lough with the MacGillicuddy
Reeks towering up beyond the silvery blue
water. The Irish Amateur Championships
(for both men and for women) have been
held in Killarney.

Above: Dancing a jig at a celebration in 1894. The main Irish step dances are the reel, light jig, heavy jig, single jig, and hornpipe. In the 1700s, dancing masters traveled to villages to teach the steps.

Enjoying Irish music and dance

Ireland is renowned for its traditional music and dancing (céilidh) and the sound of pipes and fiddles are highly evocative of the Emerald Isle, a haunting sound that seems to summon up an image of misty green hills and cosy pubs. This lilting fluid music has added a special flavor to many a movie too, including the blockbuster *Titanic*. It may take the form of pub ballads, Celtic folk music, or various traditional Irish songs, including some beautiful Gaelic ones still thriving in the western counties — some love songs have permeated down the centuries from medieval times. The music is often performed informally when friends gather together (frequently in a pub) as well as in more formal concert hall events.

Traditional and folk music may be sung unaccompanied but the musicians are usually ready and waiting to create their special Irish sound with instruments that may include the fiddle (fiddle playing is especially renowned in County Donegal), accordions called melodeon and concertina,

Right: At Listowel there are many festivals with food fairs, literary festivals, and horse racing on offer — and all provide a chance to listen to traditional Irish music in which the Irish button accordion is likely to contribute its distinctive sound as the jigs and reels set a merry pace.

Below: An Irish bodhrán drum beside a glass of stout; these goatskin drums may have derived from Celtic war drums and served Irish forces as a battle drum. Its beat would provide a cadence for the pipers and warriors alike, as well as announcing the arrival of the army.

Opposite: Local musicians make a merry sound with accordion, drum, fiddle, and guitar. Whenever Irish people gather together, there is likely to be good music playing before your beer has had time to settle.

bagpipes, wooden flute, harmonica, banjo, the bodhrán goatskin drum, and tin whistle. The music is generally fast and spirited but there are slow airs too including *sean nós* songs (featuring an unaccompanied voice singing in Irish), while the rather more sedate harp is, of course, much loved and the national symbol of Ireland. Perhaps the most famous Irish harpist was blind Turlough O'Carolan (1670–1738) who composed wonderful songs and played all over Ireland. The harp was the musical instrument of the rich and noble in ancient Ireland; harpists had to grow their nails long to be able to pluck the steel strings.

Classical tradition

Classical music is much loved here too. Musical recitals have often been held in both the cathedrals of Dublin while in 1694 the centenary of Trinity College was celebrated with a performance of Henry Purcell's *Commemoration Ode* that was composed specifically for the occasion. Handel visited Dublin in 1741 to 1742 to conduct almost 20 concerts, including two performances of his oratorio *Messiah*. Dublin's Michael Kelly was a renowned tenor who became a friend of Mozart and sang in the very first performance of *The Marriage of Figaro* in Vienna (1786). In more recent times Ireland has played host to many festivals including the Wexford Opera Festival, annual 'opera weeks' in Cork, and regular opera seasons in Limerick and Waterford. Cobh hosts carillon recitals at St Colman's Cathedral, while harpists gather from far and wide to play at the Granard Harp Festival in County Longford.

Lively traditions

Irish dance music is often very lively and encompasses reels, hornpipes, set dances and barn dances, polkas, slides, highland-style flings, waltzes, and mazurkas. Not so very long ago, the main social highlight each week was the local village dance, so many traditional dances have survived and been enjoyed ever since the 17th century. Meanwhile, the amazing skills and success of Michael Flatley's spectacular *Riverdance* (introduced as a seven-minute intermission piece in 1994's Eurovision Song Contest) and *Lord of the Dance* has brought Irish dance to an enormous international audience.

The other way to unwind is, of course, to go to the pub where live music is still very much part of the scene and provides a relaxed opportunity to hear (and, if you are good enough, join in) some lively traditional music-making and brilliant improvisation.

This page: Irish music and dancing have evolved as a living tradition through the centuries — they are a vital part of social life and entertainment in many village halls and pubs. Set and céilídh dances are often danced in squares of four couples, with variations depending on the region and local traditions.

Opposite page: Riverdance has proved an inspiration to countless young dancers. At top right, Breandan de Gallai and Joanne Doyle are poised to perform in a production of Riverdance — The Show in London. The rhythmic clickity-clackity sound of the feet, created by hard dance shoes, is an important element as well as the precise, controlled, rapid movements.

The Irish pub

So many visitors have enjoyed the very special atmosphere of traditional Irish drinking haunts that now there are 'authentic' Irish pubs in most international cities including Atlanta, Beijing, Berlin, Frankfurt, Hong Kong, Johannesburg, London, and Tokyo. But few can match the original.

The Irish word for fun, often involving drinking and music, is 'crack' or 'craic' and the pub has always been the place to find this, whether in a slick city bar on a busy street or in a country village overlooking the sea. The atmosphere is always convivial. The Irish wit is savored along with the stout.

Many of the pubs in Ireland have sumptuous Edwardian or Victorian interiors, with gleaming marble or polished mahogany bars and dark panelling. A good number offer cosy snugs. Ireland's pub history naturally stretches much farther back than Victorian times to the older coaching inns and taverns, and illegal drinking dens. There are picturesque old pubs, some with thatched roofs (like the Old Forge in Killorglin on the Ring of Kerry), traditional black and white pubs (like Belfast's 17th-century Kelly's Cellars), and multi-purpose country pubs that may also double up as the village shop or post office. Indeed, the Irish pub was often a grocery or hardware store as well as a place to drink, especially when the temperance movement impacted upon sales of spirits. The license of 'spirit-grocers' sanctioned their role as wine, tea, and spirit merchants. Often publicans served their communities as undertakers too — many still do.

Above and left: These Dublin bars — the Thomas Reid pub (above) and the Temple Bar (left) — are typical Irish pubs, busy places with attractive nostalgic features and an inviting warm atmosphere.

Back in the Middle Ages, the local tavern was where both locals and traveling merchants would take rest and refreshment, as well as ale and gin. Generally these were rough-hewn stone buildings with large fireplaces and stone, timber, or cobblestone floors with the goings-on lit by swinging oil lamps. By the 19th century, British rulers had decided to make such gathering places — where rebellion might foment — illegal so, of course, the contrary Irish ensured that they flourished all the more!

Serving drink for centuries

Dublin's one thousand or so bars may be discovered on a guided tour, including a literary pub crawl to discover the haunts of authors like Brendan Behan and to sample the fare while professional actors perform excerpts from the works of writers like James Joyce, Samuel Beckett, and Oscar Wilde. The Brazen Head is reputed to be Dublin's oldest drinking establishment — there has been a bar on this site since the 12th century — and it was once used by the Irish nationalist Robert Emmet for meetings at which he advocated rebellion against British rule. He was hanged for treason in 1803, but he is still said to be 'seen' sitting in the corner, watching out for enemies — his executioner was a regular here.

Dublin's Guinness Storehouse serves creamy pints of its famous dark brew in its rooftop bar — Ireland's highest drinking spot — and it is possible to sample the whiskey at the Old Jameson Distillery. Kavanagh's (often called the Gravediggers) in Glasnevin, Dublin, is set beside a cemetery and is named for its former busy landlord, John Kavanagh — who fathered 25 children! Its resident ghost is an elderly man in old-fashioned tweeds, who enjoys a pint at the bar before disappearing. To the north, the Abbey Tavern near Howth harbor just outside Dublin dates back to the 16th century, when it was built as a seminary for local monks.

O'Brien's Bar in Churchtown (County Cork) was a favorite haunt of Oliver Reed, the well-known actor and accomplished drinker who came to live here in 1992 and who is buried in the graveyard opposite. It is sometimes said that his ghost may be seen merrily waving to drinkers as they leave the pub.

The Antique Tavern in Enniscorthy, County Wexford, has pikestaffs and other relics from the 1798 Battle of Vinegar Hill. Kilbeggan in County Westmeath boasts the world's oldest pot still distillery, Locke's Distillery — established in 1757 but still offering the chance to sample a few brands. It is now open as a museum showing how whiskey was produced in times past. Kinsale pubs include the smuggling haunt, Spaniard Inn, Scilly, built on the ruins of an old castle.

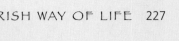

Above: Standing room only — and fairly cramped at that! This is one of many places in which to down a pint in bustling Dublin, where a constant flow of residents and visitors seek refreshment.

Left: The original Jameson Distillery in Dublin dates back to 1780. Since 1997 there has been a visitor center here to explain the Irish whiskey-making story as the various processes of malting, milling, mashing, fermenting, distilling, and maturing are divulged. There is also a chance to taste the final product in the Jameson Bar.

Right, above and below: Restaurants, bars, pubs, and cafés are especially lively and attractive when illuminated in the evening, aiming to attract customers away from the pavements and onto their outdoor terraces or through the doors. Many of the city venues are modern, slick, and sophisticated while some are highly versatile like the Café-en-Seine in Dublin (above right), which is a café by day, a pub by night and then mutates into a club venue late at night. The laid-back atmosphere makes such places very popular among local college students.

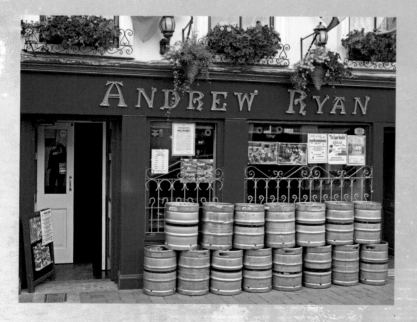

Above: A warm welcome is assured in Irish pubs where the people inside can be as lively as the paintwork outside.

Tynan's Bridge House Bar in Kilkenny has views of the castle as well as nostalgic relics from the former pharmacy and grocery store (antique scales and drawers still labeled with the names of nuts and spices). Axis Mundi in Waterford is set beside Reginald's Tower with both medieval attack exits (sallyports) and ancient Viking walls being incorporated as part of the pub fabric. Kehoe's, in the picturesque fishing village of Kilmore Quay, Wexford, is a combination of pub, parlor, restaurant, and maritime heritage center, with many treasures of the deep to admire while you enjoy the craic.

Ballycastle's family-owned House of McDonnell (established in 1766) retains the old stable blocks from its coaching-inn days and has one of the world's finest collections of traditional Irish bar mirrors (advertising various whiskey brands). It is one of a very few pubs in Ireland to retain its traditional 18th-century interior.

Oldest licensed pub

Many claim that Grace Neill's in Donaghadee, County Down, is Ireland's oldest licensed pub. It opened in 1611 as The King's Arms. There are beams made from old ship's timbers and guns that may have been used by the smugglers and horse thieves who once plotted and schemed here. Those imbibing here have included Peter the Great, Franz Liszt, John Keats, and more recently Tina Turner, and Beirut hostage Brian Keenan after his release. The pub was renamed after its former landlady who lived to be 98. She died in 1916 but her friendly ghost still appears now and then to move things about on the bar and mysteriously switch on electrical appliances.

Sean's Bar in Athlone, County Westmeath, also lays claim to the title of Ireland's oldest pub (Europe's even!), having been founded in 900 but this is a much-disputed assertion. It is tucked away behind Athlone Castle with traditional sawdust on the floor while its nooks and crannies are crammed with knick-knacks and old artefacts.

In Belfast, Irene and Nan's Bar, by the Grand Opera House, has a wonderful 1950s kitsch flavor while the National Trust-owned Crown Liquor Saloon is a Victorian riot of mosaic tiles — inside and out — with an intricately carved ceiling, comfortable snugs, gas lamps, and a long granite bar. Hidden down a cobbled alley in the cathedral quarter of Belfast is the Duke of York where Sinn Fein leader Gerry Adams once served as barman while a student. Once it quenched the thirsts of people employed in Belfast's industries and newspaper trade — as did the 1871-established Front Page bar, located opposite the *Irish News* daily newspaper. Hatfield House in Ormeau Road is almost 140 years old and

has a fine semicircular mahogany bar and elaborate decorative features created by the same craftsmen who worked on the passenger liner *Titanic*. This is a good spot to enjoy authentic Irish music at a folk night and perhaps meet a celebrity.

Whatever pub ultimately entices you through its doors, the convivial atmosphere will be one you will always remember and you will probably stay there far longer than you planned.

Above and right: Many pubs in Ireland derive their names from their owners. A Gaelic-style pub may choose a Gaelic-sounding name such as Sláinte, meaning 'Cheers.' Some pubs are named for famous Irish cities and places (The Dubliner) or authors (Samuel Beckett's and James Joyce's). Often, the illusion of a long tradition and family history is implied by adding '& Sons' to the name and many Irish pubs include initials (P.J. Foley's, for example).

THE AULD DUBLINER

LD DUBLINER

Cork Dry Gin
PUB
ENTERPRISE
AWARD
1994

THE QUAYS

GUINNESS
is good for you

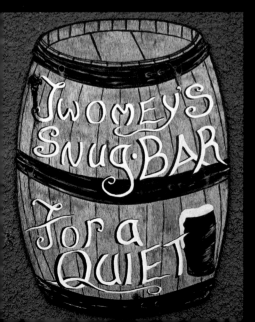

TWOMEY'S
SNUG·BAR

For a
QUIET

THE
TEMPLE
BAR

BEER GARDEN
OYSTERS
IRISH COFFEE
LIVE MUSIC DAILY

THE Whiskey

The
BRAZEN HEAD
IRELANDS · OLDEST · PUB

MUSIC AND FOOD

FUNCTION ROOM
AVAILABLE
TEL. 6795186

Live irish music 2.30pm til 2.30am

MUSICAL PUB CRAWL

EXPERIENCE DUBLIN'S FAMOUS PUBS & MUSICAL TRADITION

traditional irish music 2.30pm–2.30am

These pages: Wonderful lettering and colorful images decorate Irish pub signs, doors, windows, and many products sold within. Often they feature Celtic and Irish symbols like the Claddagh ring and the shamrock. Swinging wooden signs, blackboards, and fascia boards all exhibit ornate lettering. Back in 1393, to help his inspectors locate premises and check ale quality, King Richard II (King of England and Lord of Ireland) insisted landlords hang signs outside: 'Whosoever shall brew ale in the town with intention of selling it must hang out a sign, otherwise he shall forfeit his ale.'

Final thoughts

So this visit to Ireland finishes on a merry note, snug in the pub, listening to the music, the hum of conversation, and the shafts of Irish wit that sharpens as the whiskey and Guinness flow. Outside, beyond the steamed-up windows and brightly painted pub door is a beautiful land — a green island, a landscape of mountains, mist, and gleaming lakes, of emerald fields and hills, of soft marshes and prehistoric mysteries; a land encircled by gently shelving windswept beaches and dunes, wild and rocky seascapes, and great craggy cliffs above which birds swirl and cry. This is an isle of contrasts that has inspired a myriad legends, a rich tapestry of music, art, and literature, a land that has been the backdrop to a turbulent history — made and witnessed by a people known for their individuality, their strength and loyalty, their Irish style and humor, their poetry and their shining, smiling eyes. There are so many stories to tell and so many beautiful places in which to listen to them unfold.

Above and right: The hustle and bustle of the city and the busy pub scene melt away once your feet tread upon the springy turf and lead you to the purple haze of mountains, the glimmer of blue lake and sea, the sound of birdsong, the whirr of crickets and grasshoppers, and a gentle breeze stirring the soft green grasses. Peace descends! This is such a very different world from the clamor at the bar and yet both are Ireland. They are two faces of a multi-faceted and very beautiful land.

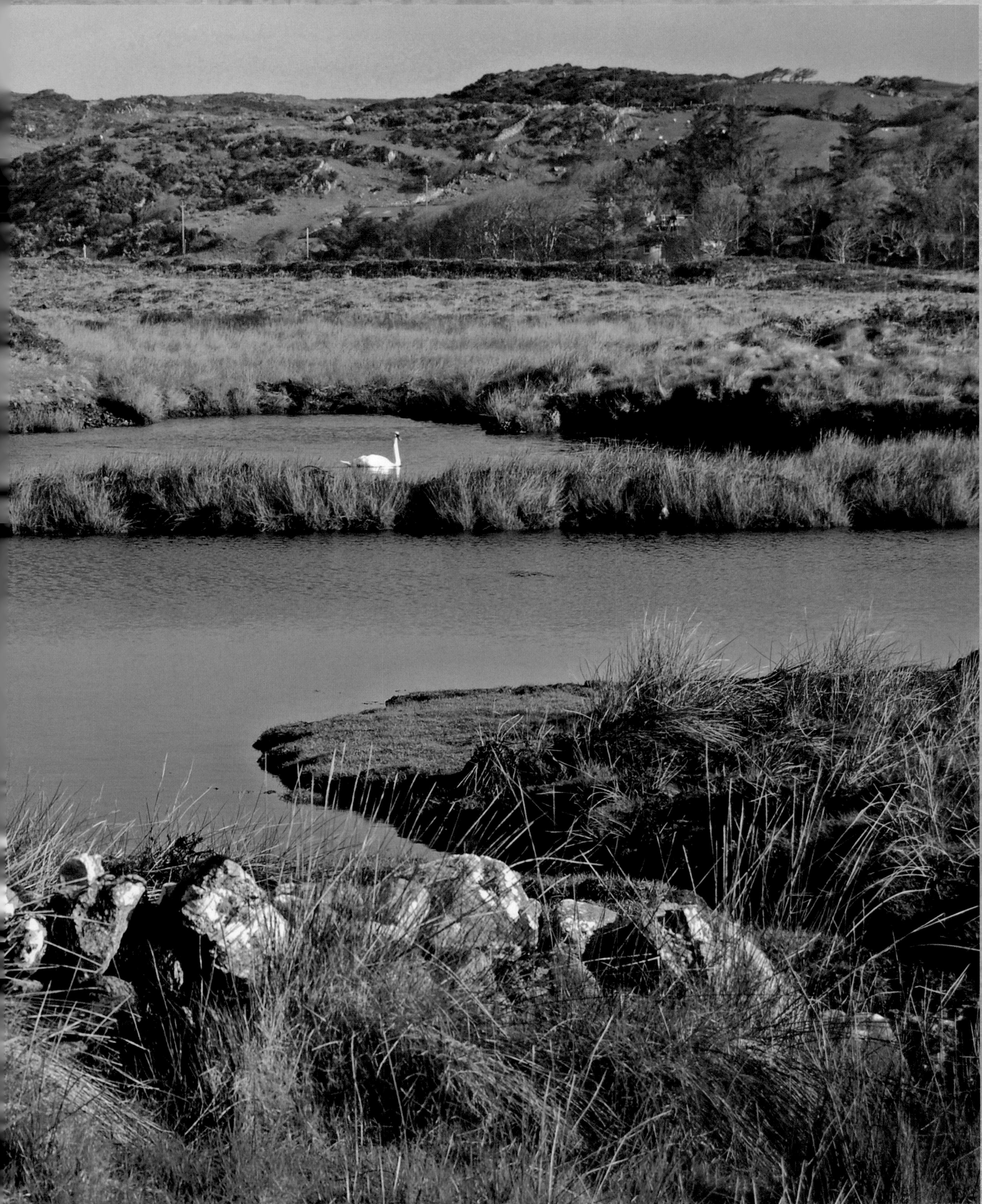

Fascinating facts and figures

History

• Newgrange passage tomb (County Meath) was built about 3200 BC, over 600 years before Egypt's Giza pyramids and around 1000 years before Stonehenge.

• The earliest hunter settlers arrived in Ireland circa 7000 BC, probably journeying across the sea from Britain.

• The Ancient Romans called Ireland 'Hibernia' … but they never conquered it.

• 13th-century Killyleagh Castle (County Down) is believed to be Ireland's oldest still-occupied castle.

• 26 counties formed the Irish Free State in 1922, while the six northeastern counties elected to remain under British jurisdiction. The Irish Free State adopted a written Constitution in 1937 and renamed itself Eire. It formally declared itself a Republic in 1949.

• Ireland was one of 12 EU nations to adopt the Euro as its currency on New Year's Day, 2002.

Geography and demographics

• After the last Ice Age, Ireland was separated from the European mainland, so naturally restricting the range of flora and fauna and denying snakes a means of entry!

• Once densely forested, Ireland was virtually denuded of tree cover in the 17th century as woodland was cleared to make way for agriculture.

• The coastline of Ireland is some 3500 miles (5600km) long.

• Ireland is the 20th largest island in the world.

• Cork is the largest and Louth the smallest county in Ireland.

• Ireland's highest peak, Carrantouhill, in Killarney (County Kerry) rises to 3415ft (1041m).

• The population of the entire island is slightly over 6 million people. Some 4,340,000 reside in the Republic of Ireland (of which 1,700,000 live in County Dublin) and 1,750,000 in Northern Ireland.

• The largest lake in Ireland is Lough Neagh at 151sq miles (392km^2).

• The River Shannon is Ireland's longest river at 240 miles (386km).

• The Burren (County Clare) is a strange landscape of limestone pavements on a 96sq miles (250km^2) plateau, originally formed some 350 million years ago.

• Eire is a constitutional democracy with its head of government being a prime minister called a *Taoiseach*, the Gaelic word for chieftain.

• Ireland's agricultural output includes barley, beef, potatoes, sugar beet, turnips, and wheat.

• Significant industries and resources include aluminum, barite, brewing, chemicals, computer software, glass and crystal, lead, machinery, passenger and commercial vehicles, pharmaceuticals, ship construction and refurbishment, silver, steel, textiles and clothing, tourism, and zinc.

• Irish (Gaelic) is spoken by some 260,000 people and used all over the island.

Irish people

• Saint Patrick, the patron saint, was born in Wales, not Ireland.

• An old legend says that while Jesus Christ will judge all other nations on Judgement Day, Saint Patrick will decide about the Irish.

• Saint Brendan is believed by some scholars to have discovered America 1000 years before Columbus.

• It is believed that Sir Walter Raleigh first introduced the potato to Ireland. He planted them at his estate at Myrtle Grove in 1596.

• In 1742 Handel's *Messiah* had its first ever public performance in Dublin at the Music Hall in Fishamble Street.

• Richard Montgomery, the first general to die in the American Revolutionary War, was born near Swords, County Dublin.

• In 1859, Irish scientist John Tyndall was the first to explain why the sky is blue. He was also one of the first scientists to identify the Earth's greenhouse effect.

• Nobel Prize winner and Trinity College, Dublin Fellow, Ernest Walton (born Dungarvan, Co Waterford) is credited with first splitting the atom in 1931 along with his colleagues Ernest Rutherford and John Cockcroft.

• Bryan Higgins of Sligo invented the first patented cement in 1789.

• John P. Holland invented the first viable, steam-powered submarine. *Fenian Ram*, launched in 1881, was his second experimental submarine — it was paid for by the Fenian Brotherhood, the nationalist movement that sought independence from Britain.

• In 1889, J.B. Dunlop, a veterinary surgeon in Belfast, invented the pneumatic tire for his son's tricycle.

• Kilkenny-born architect James Hoban designed the original White House in Washington D.C. after winning a competition in 1792. This building was destroyed by fire in 1814, but Hoban supervised its rebuilding. It was reoccupied in 1817.

• Irish actor Peter O'Toole has received the most Academy Award nominations (eight for best actor) without actually winning a single one. He has, however, received an Honorary Academy Award.

• Dubliner W.G. Wilson co-designed the world's first tank used in the Battle of the Somme during World War I.

• Oscar Wilde, Bram Stoker, Jonathan Swift, and Samuel Beckett are just a few of the many famous alumni of Dublin's Trinity College.

Opposite: Lough Derryclare, Connemara, where the landscape is inspiring albeit wild and windswept with ancient mountains long ago scoured by glaciers.

Above: Famous author William Butler Yeats (1865–1939) helped to found the Abbey Theater in Dublin in 1904. He was fascinated by Irish legends and included the giant, Cúchulainn, in several of his plays and poems.

• 20th-century Nobel Prizes for Literature have honored Irishmen George Bernard Shaw, W.B. Yeats, Samuel Beckett, and Seamus Heaney.

• Famous Irish sportsmen include soccer superstar George Best, who is a legitimate contender for the title of greatest footballer ever.

• In a 2006 survey, 35,975,855 Americans (12 percent of the total population of the United States) claimed Irish descent. Over 40 percent of all American presidents have had some Irish ancestry and 30 percent of Australians claim Irish descent.

Traditions and customs

• An old Irish wedding custom is for the wrists of the bride and groom to be tied together, which has given rise to the phrase 'tying the knot.'

• According to tradition, a wedding party should always take the longest road home from the church.

• The traditional naming convention in times gone by, in the event of a large family, was to name the first son after his father's father; the first daughter after her mother's mother; the second son after his mother's father; the second daughter after her father's mother; the third son after his father; the third daughter after her mother; the fourth son after his father's eldest brother; and the fourth daughter after her mother's eldest sister.

• Irish sailing-ship captains used to carry pebbles from Scattery Island (lying at the mouth of the River Shannon in County Clare), home of Saint Cannera, patron saint of sailors. The pebbles were considered lucky charms to protect them from shipwreck.

• The traditional unique weave patterns of individual Aran Island sweaters reputedly developed as a means of quick identification when a drowned fisherman was found.

• An old Irish hangover cure was to be buried neck-deep in wet river sand!

• The national symbol of Ireland is the Celtic harp.

Irish words and terms

• The term 'hillbilly' derived from 'billy boy,' a term used by Catholic supporters of James II to describe Protestant supporters of King William. It was used in 18th-century USA to describe Northern Ireland's Presbyterian immigrants who settled in the Appalachian Mountains.

• The term 'by hook or by crook' may have derived from Oliver Cromwell's plan to attack the town of Waterford either by taking ships around Hook Head or marching through the village of Crooke.

• The term 'Emerald Isle' first appeared in William Drennan's 1795 patriotic poem *When Erin First Rose*.

• The expression 'beyond the pale' derives from 14th-century Ireland when an area called Pale was under British control and those living outside were considered somewhat wild and lawless.

• The word 'slogan' comes from the Irish *sluagh-ghairm*, which means 'battle cry.'

• The word 'galore' comes from the Irish *go leor*, meaning 'to sufficiency' or 'plenty.'

• Dublin's name derived from the old settlement name *Dubh Linn*, which means 'Black Pool' and refers to an ancient lake there — now part of Dublin Zoo's penguin enclosure.

• The common prefixes of Mac and O found in many Irish family names derive, respectively, from the Gaelic for 'son of' and 'grandson.'

Miscellaneous

• Modern Irish is written using the Roman alphabet but the letters j, k, q, v, w, x, y, and z are missing and used only in words borrowed from foreign languages.

• Muckanaghederdauhaulia (County Galway) is the longest place name in Ireland.

• MGM's original roaring lion was born in Dublin Zoo.

• Ireland boasts Europe's highest cinema attendance.

• There have been an estimated 12,000 or so recorded shipwrecks off the coast of Ireland since 1105.

• When Oliver Cromwell invaded Ireland in 1649, he used the nave of St Patrick's Cathedral, Dublin, as a stable.

• The Normans first introduced frogs to Ireland. Swallowing a live one became a traditional cure for stomach pains.

• A 900-year old cheese was found in a Tipperary bog in 1986. Burying butter in bogs to keep it fresh was practiced in Ireland for centuries.

• Ireland has minimal coal deposits, even though it's just 60 miles (97km) from Wales, one of the world's richest coal fields.

• The first recorded horse race at Ireland's famous racecourse, the Curragh, took place in 1727 although the site had been used for races long before that. The Curragh offers the highest quality of flat racing in Ireland and all five Irish classics are run there.

• The tallest ever identical twins were the Knipe Brothers, born in County Derry in 1761 who reportedly grew to a height of 7ft 2in (2.18m).

Opposite: Ireland's lush green grass and verdant hills gave rise to the term 'the Emerald Isle,' first coined in William Drennan's 1795 poem When Erin First Rose. *Erin is Ireland's old poetic name.*

Above: On Inishbofin Island, Cromwell's Barracks carve a stark jagged outline. The penal colony housed many a captured Catholic clergyman awaiting transportation to faraway lands like the West Indies. One bishop was tied to Bishop's Rock and left to drown as the tide rose.

• Trinity College, Dublin is Ireland's oldest university, it boasts the largest research library in Ireland. As the legal deposit library for Ireland and the United Kingdom it is entitled to a copy of every book published and consequently receives over 100,000 new items every year.

• A 'proper' pint of Guinness should be poured in 'Guinness time' — roughly three-quarters of the pint is pulled, and then left to settle. Once the creamy head has fully formed, the glass is then topped up. This convention is often disregarded outside Ireland, which is one reason why people think Guinness tastes better in Ireland.

Irish quotes

• *There is no language like the Irish for soothing and quieting.* (John Millington Synge)

• *You know it's summer in Ireland when the rain gets warmer.* (Hal Roach)

• *I am a drinker with a writing problem.* (Brendan Behan)

• *I spent 90 percent of my money on women and drink. The rest I wasted.* (George Best)

• *Those who drink to forget, please pay in advance.* (Notice in a Cork bar)

• *If you are lucky enough to be Irish, then you are lucky enough.* (Traditional Irish saying)

INDEX